Céline Semaan

A Woman is a School

Published by Slow Factory Books
for Collective Liberation © 2024

Slow Factory Books for Collective Liberation
© 2024

First Edition, 2024

Edited by Colin Vernon, Suzanne Potts and
Farah-Silvana Kanaan
Copy edited by Jeff Braucher
Proofread by T. Liem
Designed by Maya Moumne
Cover Artwork by Céline Semaan
Printed and bound by Ingram

ISBN: 979-8-218-43707-7

www.slowfactory.earth

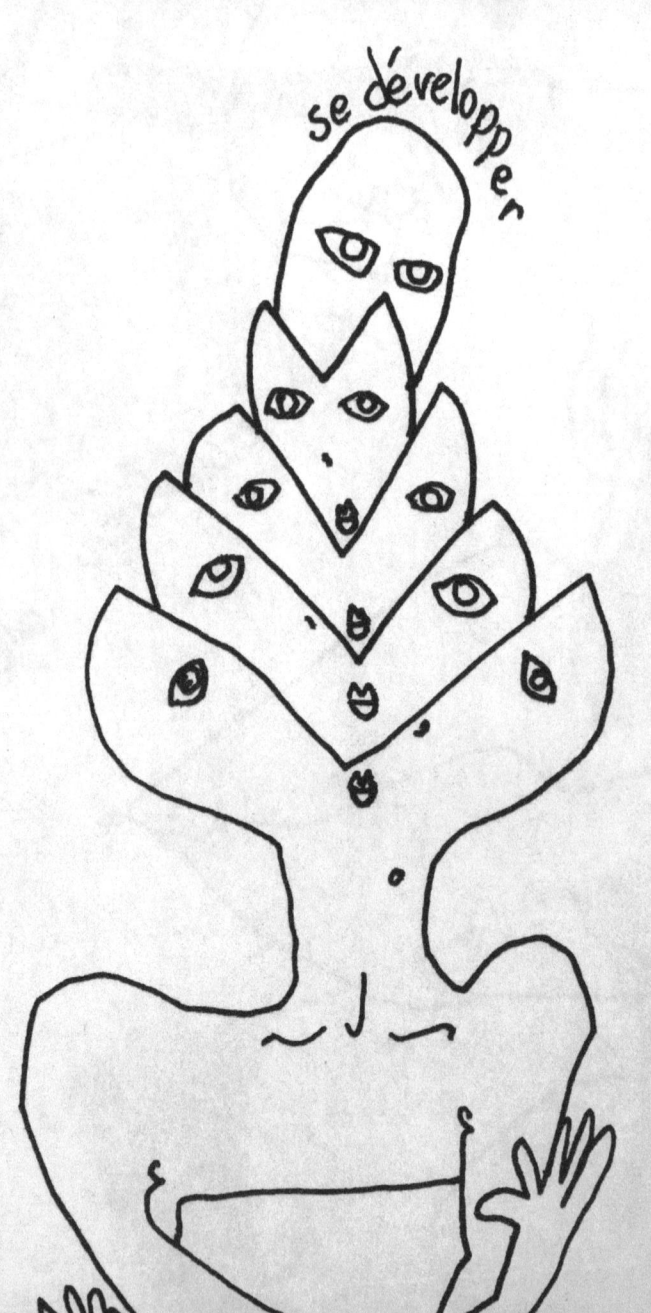

This book is dedicated to my daughters and
mothers of the Global South who
understand that stories are data with a soul.

A collection of stories holding the blueprint
on how to thrive.

**"A woman is a school,
if you teach her, you teach
an entire generation."**

— from *The Light in Her Eyes* (2011)
dir. Julia Meltzer & Laura Nix

To the divine feminine within all of us.

To my children Sila Grey & Luma Rosie and to all the women and girls of the Global South and their sacred knowledge.

Deep gratitude to my partner and husband Colin (Collis Browne) Vernon, to my mother Ghada Semaan and her whole lineage, my father Samir Semaan and his lineage, my grandmothers Albertine Samaha and Souad Semaan, and my great-grand mothers Téta Marie Aoun and Shams Semaan, my sister Laeticia Semaan Aoun and brother Cyril Semaan, my aunties Mona Azzi, Hala Samaha, and Samira Semaan, Samia Semaan, my dearest soul sisters Anita Kopacz and Yvonna Kopacz-Wright, LexyRose Scott, Nidia Temple, Syntyché Francella, Laura Chung, my editors Suzanne Potts and Farah-Silvana Kanaan, my Slow Factory team Paloma Rae, Nicole Nimri, Daleen Saah, Yassa Almokhamad-Sarkisian, Joshua Potash, Afeef Nessouli, and to my dear friend and forever designer Maya Moumne.

To my people in Lebanon, Palestine, and Syria who deserve to live free and sovereign. End the occupation.

Definition: A Woman

Woman, noun: To be a human who identifies as a woman regardless of the nation-states' definition of femininity and without limitation of gender norms imposed and established under patriarchal colonial rule.

Contents

INTRODUCTION
In the Name of the Revolution   **10**

CHAPTER ONE
Open All the Roads   **20**

CHAPTER TWO
Of Sacred Rebellion and Joyful Defiance   **54**

CHAPTER THREE
Heal Your Mother's Mother: On Radical Care   **88**

CHAPTER FOUR
International Solidarity: The Water is Sacred   **118**

CHAPTER FIVE
Global South, Baby   **160**

CHAPTER SIX
Fashion and Politics   **194**

CHAPTER SEVEN
Radical Generosity   **226**

CHAPTER EIGHT
Unlearning War   **254**

CHAPTER NINE
Radical Imagination   **278**

*There is a psychological phenomenon that
consists in the belief that the world will open to the
extent to which frontiers are broken down.*

~ Frantz Fanon ~

In the Name of the Revolution

"Sisso!" my mother singsongs, "Sassouna!"

I am around three or four years old, dancing on top of a table in true Lebanese fashion. I shake my tiny hips to my grandmother Souad's singing, entertaining the adults while my great-uncle plays the oud and sings alongside her. As I belly dance on the table, I am transforming my family's pain into joy. The adults gather around me, their laughter and clapping encouraging me to dance more fervently, so, like a dervish in a trance, I dance. The membrane protecting us and surrounding us is now fortified. Nothing will break us. Nothing will get to us. Not even the bomb that has just fallen near our building. We are invincible.

"Sisso!" My mother's voice, now distressed, pulls me out of my trance. Like a siren, it reverberates through my small body and gets stored in my cells as the sound of terror, a sound too close to death. This vibration holds onto me from within.

I realize later in life that this vibration changed when my family decided finally to flee.

My father is granted refugee status and temporarily (or so we hope) leaves my mother, my sister, and me in Beirut. He departs for Montreal with only a modest sum in his pocket and a few items of clothing to sell. A few months later, my mother receives a letter containing the necessary paperwork to reunite us. We are uprooted from our native land and cast into the unknown, leaving the rest of our extended family behind.

Once in Montreal my parents insist that we forget all about our journey and our past. We are in a new land and a new life, and we are discouraged from looking back. All past memories are wiped clean, including the language I speak and even the name I'm used to.

My mother hands me a piece of paper and a pen and says, "Write your name."

I protest in Arabic.

She interrupts me in French and insists, "Write your name."

On the piece of paper I write "Céline" again and again, a hundred times until the letters align properly and my tiny fingers manage to control every curve the pen makes. That name is a passport, a way to blend in and to be accepted in the Global North.

My mother grew up in Beirut in the aftermath of French colonial rule and understood then that her name could not be pronounced by the colonial invaders. She recognized their limited ability to create sounds with their stubborn tongues and lips, the sounds intrinsic to her language, identity, and heritage. She promised herself that we, her children, would not have to suffer the mockery and ridicule she suffered. We would be given names that would dupe the oppressors into believing we were one of them. Our colonial names, adopted out of survival and defiant courage, would also provide us with name-given entitlement.

I have recounted these stories time and time again.

I was born in Lebanon during the war, in the same year our president and his daughter were murdered in a car explosion. Five years later we fled to Montreal. We lived there as refugees for nine years, and in the mid-1990s, returned to the apocalyptic postwar hell that Beirut had become.

Whenever we look back at history to try to understand our roots, our origins, our traditions and culture, we often find ourselves face to face with trauma. This trauma is a massive energetic barrier unwittingly kept up by the generations who have suffered deeply under the hands of oppressors. The barrier of trauma grows thick and strong and impenetrable over the years; it becomes a mountain so intimidating that few dare attempt to overcome it. Taboo, shame, disgrace, pain, tears, wounds, and family secrets constitute each and every rock in this Mountain of Trauma.

In the geographies of our spirits, the barrier of trauma, the Mountain, grows during and after inhumane violent events perpetrated by oppressive colonizing regimes. These events destabilize the balance and harmony within an existing community. Ironically, the Mountain actually serves to protect the stories of the past that preserve native or Indigenous wisdom—the very wisdom the oppressors are so terrified of. Any person who might dare express or embody such traditional knowledge suffers the wrath of the oppressors who make sure they meet a terrible death. This death becomes known to all in the community and then serves as a warning: Do not challenge the oppressor. Consequently, the survivors of this inhumane violence make sure to protect the Mountain that serves as a shield. The tragedy is that this shield also denies the community access to their own sacred knowledge.

Nevertheless, each successive generation will inevitably attempt to push through the rocky edifice of the Mountain. Eventually these rebellious youth, like irrepressible seedlings, penetrate the walls of the Mountain through cracks and crevices, and a new generation of seedlings grow into vines that weave past with present with future. The younger generation, in spite of oppression and the constant threat of violence and death, are fierce and insist on blossoming as a refutation of the war waged against them, their families, their communities, and their ancestors. Often, it is the children who—having faced death, destruction, and loss at early ages by being born into and raised under colonial rule, and having been terrorized by years of war and chaos—develop heightened senses and extraordinary gifts of resistance and resilience.

This is my memoir—a selection of my personal stories intertwined with the personal stories of family, friends, and mentors, along with a political critique of the ravages of colonialism, patriarchy, capitalism, and white supremacy. Most significantly, my memoir is a passionate philosophical exploration of the often dismissed and discredited ancient Indigenous knowledge mostly transmitted through the sacred, intuitive, nature-based, heart-centered, body-aware teachings of women following an oral tradition.

My intention is to offer an alternative to what the Western academic institutions and media offer. Those institutions are basically an extension of colonial belief systems and power dynamics that intentionally other the vast majority of people living on this planet and justify exploitation, war, torture, rampant pollution, and insidious as well as overt oppression as necessary evils. The stories in this book are gathered with the purpose of creating a body of work focused on tales of radical creative resistance and unfathomable courageous resilience.

I explore the discredited knowledge that is passed down from women to girls through culture and tradition by those who belong to the Global Majority[1]—knowledge that inspired me to write *A Woman Is a School*. I wanted to document and record this important form of education that is endangered and often erased.

My responsibility as a Lebanese Arab woman writer is to bear witness, to collect oral stories—small tales of resistance—that would otherwise be forgotten. The events I witnessed as a first-generation war survivor have built the interconnected and compounding layers of understanding that flow out of me into concrete methodologies designed to contribute to the already vast body of work that has been built by writers, poets, and philosophers such as Fanon, Said, Ture, Wynter, and Césaire, to name a few. The everyday resistance of the souls who are creatively refusing to capitulate to the persistent and oppressive colonial aesthetics and systems are the souls who are building new ways of being.

This book aims to inspire, ignite, and awaken within a joyful, productive, healing energy that when put into action creates a new paradigm by solidifying an equitable reality and a new level of consciousness born of a reconnection to Indigenous ideals. I believe in this vision in spite of the stubbornness of colonial thought and the illusion of patriarchy and white supremacy that has been sold to us over and over again through every single conduit of the media machine.

We are collectively the school we have been waiting for. We are here to connect, to teach, and empower each other with the tools we've always had available within. This book is here to embolden you to rise, shine, and become—to establish the visions you have received about how things ought to be. This book is giving you the permission you always thought you needed to affirm your knowledge. We hold far more wisdom than all the schools combined. We are the school.

NOTES

1. Global Majority is a term that includes Black, brown, Indigenous, and minority ethnic folks—or nonwhite folks—who together constitute the majority of cultures that are erased, discredited, and oppressed by white supremacy and capitalist colonial military occupation around the world.

A Woman
is a School

CHAPTER I

Open
All
the
Roads

Cassette #1: "Li Beirut"

Fairuz laments in her godly voice. Her mourning for her country crystallizes into a sound that recalls the purity of church bells. Its vibrations move through the souls of every single person displaced by this unholy war, transforming us all into saints.

The Road Most Traveled

There is an expression about the road less traveled. But it's the road most traveled that fundamentally defines us. The very first road we ever travel begins with dreadful rejection, an utterly painful feeling of loss. We experience the trauma of being rejected as we are expelled from our first home, our mother. The body that has held us for those first months of life forces us to create a path out of it, but this rejection is necessary for mutual survival. Often, the first child has a harder time finding a way out. If the birth is vaginal, the child has to open a new road where there was no path before. It is a terrifying ordeal for both child and mother.

My pregnant great-grandmother, barely a teenager at the time, managed to push my grandfather out of her body with the help of midwives who'd traveled by foot through many small rural villages to be by her side. Although there are few documents left about how the midwives delivered our ancestors, our oral tradition has relayed information about their techniques. Ropes were tied around the mother so the midwives could hold onto her as she pushed the child out; traditional herbs were used as medicine to calm the mother and induce labor if necessary; and physical manipulation was used to assist the mother in birthing the child. A midwife would insert her hands into the vaginal tunnel and pull the child out while the mother wailed.

And so, my grandfather's journey began with the first universal trauma of rejection that birth inevitably creates. Little did he know that just a few years later he would be rejected yet again by the woman who gave him life. This rejection was a consequence of love. But not for him or for his father. His mother had fallen in love with a young man and decided to leave her husband and son for him. The separation was unexpected and brutal for my grandfather.

In many family sagas, a wall of shame is built so high that it can take a few generations to uncover the truth. It wasn't until I was in my late twenties that I overheard my sister and mother quietly talking about this particular story. I began bombarding them with questions; I had no idea that my grandfather had grown up without his mother.

"The entire village knew what she'd done," my sister shared. "How could she? She must have had no heart. She was so vain!"

My mother added, "I could hear the women in the village lamenting: 'Ya 3ayb el shoum,[2] at her age? How could he want her, she was no longer a virgin! What a shame. What a shame'."

What my mother and sister failed to mention was

that my great-grandmother was a child bride to begin with, and when she left her husband and son to follow her heart, she wasn't even twenty years old. Throughout my grandfather's life, this early ruthless rejection grew into an ironclad resentment to the extent that it became impossible to get him to talk about his mother. He couldn't forgive her and never wanted to see her again. He, in turn, had decided to reject her.

In 1935, five years after my grandfather's mother left, his father, overcome with shame, decided to withdraw him from school at only ten years old so he could go to work. My grandfather Labib and his father, Abu-Labib, began working as a team building roads from their village in the Metn region of Lebanon to the capital city of Beirut. My grandfather would now open new roads with his father from early morning until late at night. While he was busy creating physical paths for others, metaphorical ones had been shut in his face. A formal education had been taken away from him, and his last day of school left him grief-stricken as he adored learning. He was an exemplary student, and his teachers tried in vain to convince his father to change his mind because they saw great potential in Labib. But Abu-Labib insisted that hard work would provide his son with a sense of purpose and direction that an education could not.

Labib, like his father, was to live the simple but tough life of a "real" man, with his back bent in the sun and his hands digging through the soil. Building things: This was an ideal of masculinity that extolled the virtues of hard physical labor. A real man rises from the ground. So, at the tender age of ten, Labib had lost both the woman who had given him life and the school that would have taught him about life.

From then on, my grandfather's life became all about creating roads. Building roads at that time demanded unimaginable endurance and stamina. Although some light machinery was used, the job was overwhelmingly physical. I remember my grandfather recounting how his entire body would be covered in reddish-brown dust, and how he was so used to the aching and the sweltering sun and the dust that the days, months, and years overlapped in his memory. This was a time and place where physical endurance was the measure of a man's value.

Not being allowed to go to school did not stop Labib from dreaming of becoming an engineer one day, of building ships that could go all the way to the moon. He kept his dreams secret so he would stay motivated to continue learning on his own. He was born gifted, with talents in illustration, writing, and turning visions into reality. When his workday was over, instead of relaxing and going to bed early after yet another day of grueling labor, Labib would carve the bits of wood he'd collected from his worksite and turn them into miniature pieces of furniture, buildings, cars, and spaceships. Meanwhile, he would imagine what his life would have been like had he been allowed to stay in school. His big dream was to be an engineer, but without school or any degrees, all he could do was get his hands on books and read, read, read, as if his life depended on it. Through these books, he taught himself all he needed to know to become the closest thing to an engineer: an architect.

Only a few years before Labib was born, France seized control of Lebanese territories after the San Remo Conference.[3] The French occupation was viciously violent. Although there had been various invasions of Lebanon by outside forces for many centuries—since the early 1200s— the post-World War I French colonial incursion was incalculably destructive to the region. It was similar to the British Mandate for Palestine, which devalued Indigenous culture and imposed Eurocentrism on the local population while extracting oil and other desirable resources.

The segregation of Arab communities was one of many collective traumas we suffered as a result of the European "divide and conquer" playbook. In 1920 the French officially took possession of Syria and Greater Lebanon following the establishment of the control of three undefined, previously Ottoman Empire colonies in the Middle East: Palestine, Syria, and Mesopotamia. Leaders of the Global North concluded that the region wasn't fit for independence and was therefore in need of European "patronage." The division of the land resulted in more than a century of war and conflict up until today since the land wasn't the Europeans' to arbitrarily divide and occupy.

The French implemented their formula for control in Lebanon—as they had done elsewhere—by exercising authority over the Lebanese educational institutions and cultural traditions. Education and culture are powerful tools of social control, and during this period the French government established over four hundred French schools where members of the Lebanese ruling class would be educated.[4] The French educational system would eventually extend to the majority of the population, forcing the Lebanese people to speak French and learn the European way of life. Traditional clothes were mocked by the European interlopers and then eventually shunned by the Lebanese people. The idea that Indigenous culture belonged only to ignorant peasants was propagated by the French, who also insisted that to be sophisticated and modern meant adopting European culture and mannerisms.

These oppressive, external aesthetics would soon become a dominant force. Colonial propaganda insists on a social hierarchy that places the white man at the top of the pyramid and uses modernity as its weapon of erasure and control. The closer a human is to the land, the lower his value. Peasants and farmers dressed in traditional clothes were considered to be vulgar and beneath the city merchants and office workers who dressed in suits. The colonial powers that be used these demeaning psychological strategies to deny the Indigenous people of Lebanon access to and sovereignty over their own land. Those who worked the land were considered "soiled," both literally and metaphorically.

The Lebanese people who grew up in the French school system during the French Mandate period, and even up until the education of my parents, are what I call the "lost generations"—those who internalized the idea that the colonizer was in fact superior in all ways and was sent to save them from themselves. Colonized peoples navigate the colonial mindset that was forced upon them in different ways.

I have seen two distinct sides to the colonized mind. There are those who become proud of their proximity to the colonizer; they aspire to be like the colonizer and to become conquerors themselves. They externalize this by expressing a strong need to dominate others, even their own kin. Conversely, there are those who share a profound hatred toward their colonizer, but instead of mobilizing against the occupying forces, they take it out on their brothers. They believe they are fighting the colonizer, yet they destroy and fight each other. Identifying with a tight and factional concept of tribe, they ultimately serve the occupation by falling into the divide-and-conquer tactic, which is what happened in Lebanon. This tactic, and its consequences, persisted until recently.

Deep down both types want to dominate. Both have forgotten the Indigenous values of living in harmony with nature and each other. Both uphold colonial values and support segregation and division. Both prioritize status, proximity, and access over compassion, connection, and sacredness. Colonized people often become the colonizer and end up betraying themselves and their own people. This isn't something that is specific to Lebanon. This is a universal phenomenon. This is what colonialism does to its subjects.

Being taken out of school protected Grandfather Labib from becoming either of these two types. Because he was not subjected to a colonial education in the French schools, he didn't experience the internalized division that a colonial education creates. Though he hadn't wanted to leave school, this turn of events ultimately allowed him to preserve his ethnic identity and dignity, free from the Europeanization his compatriots were subjected to. His French was rudimentary—he knew just enough to stay out of trouble—but overall, his entire life was lived and expressed in Arabic. He remained whole. Grounded. And most important, sovereign. This is why his spirit gave him the power to achieve so much in his own way.

Grandfather Labib was a literal trailblazer, creating roads where there had been none before. He learned early on that he had to rely on himself, and to have an unshakable faith in his ability to learn. He had to become acquainted with himself on an intimate level and to know his gifts and his purpose. He knew how to honor the sacred and how to transform his pain into creative action. The roads he created serve as an invitation for all of us to become everything we ever dreamed of in spite of rejection, abandonment, and external pressures to conform or capitulate to the control of another.

To even begin to know ourselves requires a level of self-acceptance that may be difficult to find. Yet some, like my grandfather, manage to do so despite an avalanche of additional hurdles. He would talk of alchemy—the alchemy of transforming suffering into passion—a concept he gathered from reading Khalil Gibran, Abu Nuwas, Al-Mu-tanabbi, and Rumi, his favorite poets. This is the kind of wisdom we can only learn through experience. My grand-father's life is an example of alchemy in action, in over-coming betrayal and turning wounds into muscles, finding a rhythm through discipline, and eventually transforming vision into reality.

All this family history has informed my understand-ing of the world. As I've grown, and as I learned these stories over the course of my life, I've connected them to my own struggles and patterns.

From time to time I find myself going through re-jection and betrayal. Over the years I have gathered a collection of rejection letters from prestigious schools, foundations, and funders. I even have a list of people who would happily watch me fall, crash, and burn. Many doors have closed on me, sometimes all at once, and people I considered family or partners went from uncomfortable levels of flattery to sworn enemies within a year.

When you open up roads and create a path that didn't exist before, you become a trailblazer, but you can also end up disturbing those who fear change and are desper-ate to hold onto the past. But those of us who are driven to explore and create new paths, to trailblaze and to exist in service to all of humanity, do so for everyone's best interest. Our purpose is to create access for others, to con-tribute to collective liberation by opening the road and inviting all who are willing to take the journey toward self-awareness and personal transformation.

A Long Unexpected Journey

I was running behind my mother who was carrying my little sister. I was carrying all the plush toys I could fit in my short five-year-old arms. My mother had warned me that I couldn't possibly carry all of them. But I was determined to at least try. Through my tears I had trouble keeping track of her; clearly we were late for something. The plush toys one by one fell out of my clutch, leaving a trail of soft breadcrumbs. Except this was not a path I would be able to retrace to find my way home. Nor was this a fairy tale.

I glanced back and saw my favorite plush toys lying abandoned on the glossy floor of the Beirut airport while people rushed by, unconsciously kicking them out of their way. My heart squeezed tears out of my eyes. I looked ahead and spotted my mother's boots, pulled tightly over her denim jeans, and ran to catch up. She clutched my baby sister who was wrapped securely in a handknit blanket. I ran as fast as I could to reach them as more plush toys fell, my arms tired and aching. Exhausted and scared, I could only focus on moving forward. By the time I finally reached my mother, I was out of breath and only one toy remained cradled in my arms, a little gray elephant. We boarded the plane, my mother's face shrouded in a veil of tears. Holding my sleeping sister, she took her seat. I nestled next to her, placed my head in her lap and drifted off to sleep.

My journey from Beirut with my one remaining stuffed gray elephant was another sort of trailblazing.

Being forced by rejection into blazing new paths turns out to run in my family. When I was five, my family and I were forced to flee Beirut. It was 1987, twelve years into a horrifying civil war that had Lebanon in a physical and emotional choke hold, when my sister and I left with my mother (my grandparents, aunties, and other family members weren't able to come with us) after we obtained refugee status. We were sent to the United States to reunite with my father, who was already in Canada. My father had lobbied for a family reunification, but nothing had been approved yet, which meant that we had to be escorted to Montreal from the United States border, where we were left stranded for hours, uncertain if the plan would even work.

I still have and cherish the photo we had to take for our family passport to apply for refugee status. My mother's black eyeliner, her big curly hair, leather jacket, and perfectly defined lips, colored a magnificent dirty rose. My sister and I are both wearing handknit wooly sweaters, red and white, in imitation of Mickey Mouse's iconic outfit, which my mother had worked so hard on. My hair, also big and curly, sharply contrasts with my shy smile. My sister has only a few hairs peeking out from her head; she was not even one year old. She looks straight into the camera, absolutely stunned. This photo of us would crown the passport that led us to safety. How was it possible that we reached the border without a formal status and made it into the country? It was the result of a lot of pressure from my father, the efforts of my mother, and even an important contribution by my tiny self.

After we had spent agonizingly long hours locked away from the world in a small room, my mother suddenly turned to me and whispered in Arabic: "Go lie on the floor and cry loudly. Go crazy." Without a second thought, I obliged. I had been holding everything in anyway; I was so tired and scared. I cried and freaked out in the middle of the floor while my mother called for the officers to witness our collective desperation. My baby sister had a fever; she too was crying. My mother was beyond hysterical.

The Canadian officers went back and forth between our room and where my father was. He was protesting, insisting he would not leave the building without us. And we were exhausted and unsure of what was going to happen to us. I cried, sitting on the floor until I couldn't anymore. At midnight, after we had waited for what felt like an entire day and night, we were asked to go to a nearby hotel and wait there until the next day when we would be officially admitted to the country. My parents did not believe the officer, but we were forced to exit the premises. I ran into my father's arms, and he carried me to the hotel. While my sister and I slept, my parents spent the night awake holding each other. The tears would not come anymore, their eyes had completely run dry.

I have no memory of the early morning when the border officers made good on their promise to let us all into Canada legally and permanently, thus opening the road for the next several years and forever changing the course of my life. For many years my family would not speak of this time, preferring to erase this part of our story. Whenever I would bring it up, ask questions, or remember moments of my early childhood during the war—flashbacks of scenes of us running to the shelters, scenes of us at the airport fleeing, the traumatic family reunification ordeal—my mother would demand with great authority that I stop. She'd insist that nothing had happened, that we must not talk about it to anyone. So, I would stop. But I couldn't erase these memories. In a way, our country had rejected us and forced us to open a new road for ourselves. Our people had betrayed themselves by turning their country into a war zone. The colonized became the colonizer, and all of us turned against one another, fighting until death trying to dominate each other. The white man's idea of a "pure race" was nothing but poison, polluting our people's minds and land.

That ideology, of course, predates the French Mandate. Europeans have disrupted our region for a thousand years. Our people were groomed to betray each other. Most recently, during the civil war, they murdered and kidnapped their own kin, bombed their land, and poisoned their water. The war reinforced the mountain of shame that traps stories behind it and overwhelmed us with dread and rendered us (temporarily) silent. But just as nature cannot be contained, neither can our stories. Just like roots, they pierce through concrete, forging new paths forward. Like water, our stories flow through the mountain into the creeks of our collective imagination. We survive in order to tell these stories.

During our exile, my mother sent cassette tapes on which she recorded stories for my grandparents and aunties back home. She'd hide in her room and share her secrets into the tape recorder. We often heard her break down and cry. Finally finished, she would step out of her bedroom looking composed and elegant in every way. She'd call us one by one to come in and record a message on the tape. We sang songs and answered her questions, which prompted the telling of elaborate and entertaining childish stories. The tapes would then be sent with someone traveling from Montreal to Beirut. After my relatives listened to our news, they would record over the tapes we sent and send them back to us with travelers returning to Montreal. My parents would grab the tapes and lock themselves in their room to listen. Again, we heard their sobs, but also their laughter.

When we first arrived in Montreal, mere months after we had fled, I was enrolled in school. Up until this time I spoke and read almost exclusively in Arabic, and the little French I knew was very different from the dialect spoken in Quebec. A few days before school began, my mother taught me to write my name on a piece of paper. I had to write "Céline" in cursive, over and over again. I was five years old, writing my name again and again, my mother standing over me, continuously reprimanding my imperfections. I had to try harder and be better. I remember being forced to write my name for hours, which led me to have an accident in my underwear, which then led to a spanking. The name on the paper continued to be poorly written, my fragile five-year-old fingers trying their best.

During my first weeks of school, I spoke only Arabic. At one point, excited to share, I stood on a desk and began to dance in our traditional way, called *baladi*. I wanted to share my story and the things I knew. I was admonished by the teacher and humiliated by the other students, who mercilessly mocked me. My teacher reported my "disruptive" behavior to my mother, who instead of comforting me became mad at me for what she saw as a severe transgression on my part.

All this contributed to my feeling that I wasn't safe anywhere. Every night I had to catch up on my homework, study, and read, trying to make up for the years of learning I had missed. No matter how hard I tried, I would always fall behind. At school I couldn't sit still. I was diagnosed by the school counselors with ADHD and hyperactivity. I was scolded by my mother because she refused to accept these new terms, these diagnoses that were supposed to describe my behavior. As far as she was concerned, I was just a spoiled child who needed to be disciplined.

Every day I felt disdain emanating from the students and teachers alike. Aside from deliberately butchering my last name at every opportunity and making fun of my extremely curly hair, I was also despised for not being able to sit still, memorize, or focus. Teachers loved complaining about me to my mother, who unfailingly took their side. She would then unleash her wrath on me. Even at such a young age, I hated the establishment with my whole being. The way they forced us to sit still in chairs all day felt unbearable.

This new life provided such a stark contrast to the life I'd led in Lebanon. Lebanon wasn't all wonderful. There was the daily stress of living through war, finding shelter during the raids, and eventually fleeing the country and leaving everything and (almost) everyone I knew and loved behind. But there was a way of being, growing, and learning that gave me permission to be the woman I am today. All my early "teachers" lived in a magical place outside of the school system. They were the everyday "wisdom keepers" that were (and still are) braving oppression despite the colonial systems that were attempting to purposefully erase and discredit them for their knowledge, their truth, and their innate grace. They were my grandmothers and aunties and neighbors, the women who looked after me and told me their stories and taught me.

On Code-Switching

At home, safely inside the walls that delineated the borders of our private world, we lived and practiced our traditional culture. The culture we shared in my home contrasted radically with the culture I was exposed to on the street, at school, and through my new friends. This is a classic immigrant story, I suppose, as I have heard this sentence uttered a million times by every single migrant, refugee, immigrant, and expat I've ever encountered. We all share this inside-outside understanding and the innate survival instinct of "code-switching." The way we spoke inside the home was different from the way we spoke outside the home. I learned this early on after we landed in Montreal.

Code-switching helped me avoid getting myself into bad situations—either a severe punishment at home for being disrespectful or a punch in the gut on the playground for not belonging. Learning through our collective survival is key. In our neighborhood we were looked down on by white families. It was made clear to us, and sometimes even written on the windows of my father's store, that we were "dirty Arabs," "immigrants," and that we ought to "go home." In both a symbolic and a very visceral way, our own country had abandoned us and there wasn't a home to go to.

We were forced to leave our home; we were betrayed by our own people who had turned against each other in a quest to dominate and appeal to international forces putting our country in a choke hold. Our safety was at risk; we left our homeland to open a new road of possibilities for ourselves and, consequently, for many other Lebanese families who would use our place as a home on their way to citizenship in Canada. My father opened the roads that led us to the belly of the beast: the Global North, the West, the so-called civilized world. The goal destination for war survivors. The Babylon of all colonial ideals and ideas of comfort. It is where we would have a real future.

Hundreds of millions of people look at the Global

North from where they stand in the Global South—deeply exploited, unbalanced, and at the brink of climate collapse—and think the same way: this is the road to safety. It is understandable, this desire to leave home for a better world. My parents ended up returning home after close to a decade abroad. As soon as the first ceasefire was declared, they packed their belongings, sold everything at a loss, and returned to their land where they are still trying to live despite the ongoing climate, the political and economic unrest.

Staying there is still a challenge even decades later because of ongoing aggression from the Occupation of Palestine, economic and political corruption in Lebanon, and the growing environmental climate crisis. In our region, plurality of culture and ethnicity (the idea of sustaining multiple perspectives and cultures at the same time) has always been the norm, since our peoples came from different tribes that spoke multiple languages and worshiped different forms of the Divine. Nonetheless, these different cultures agreed that education was a sacred value. For instance, the study of nature and the cosmos helped explain or predict natural phenomena and thus was considered sacred. For us, education has always been interconnected with agricultural knowledge, knowledge that was often shared through oral stories as well as scriptures and almanacs.

Many of the recipes we continue to cook today are thousands of years old—some of which can be found in the first cookbook ever created in the Arab world.[5] It is a

wonderful collection of historical stories, culture, knowledge of nature, and the deep understanding of our land
and natural elements. Contrary to colonial claims, our area
was always a place where the transmission of knowledge
and innovation were of paramount importance. Archaeological evidence shows that the first schools in the history of mankind were established in Mesopotamia and
ancient Egypt.[6]

The Levant also witnessed the invention of the first
writing systems and the world's first phonetic alphabet,
the Phoenician alphabet. For almost three centuries Beirut housed a school of Roman Law, and its scholars were
called upon to write a legal code in the 6th century AD.
This body of law is still at the core of many current legal
systems globally. New educational institutions emerged
in Abbasid Baghdad and in all other major Muslim urban
centers. These schools and massive libraries were repos-
itories of knowledge and centers of education. Many of
the founding notions of modern philosophy, science, and
technology were developed there. In the 19th century the
small rural schools of Mount Lebanon were turned into
modern institutions and played a key role in the Arab Nah-
da (Renaissance) of the late 19th-early 20th century, training a generation of thinkers and actors of change. These
were things I learned from my friend Charles al-Hayek,
who endeavors to safeguard our heritage through his body
of work and through education.

Lebanese folks knew that our ancient, traditional body
of knowledge was more extensive than the European rulers'

knowledge base; however, we also knew that learning their language would help us find our way faster in their expanding world. Learning has always been such a source of pride for our people, so we learn efficiently. What qualifies us as avid learners is our sense of humility in the face of the unknown and the shared understanding that knowledge is sacred. Learning our ancestral knowledge enhanced our ability to adapt.

Within that paradigm exists its contradiction, in that there is also a place for refusal. Unlearning is as much learning as it is self-preservation and sovereignty. Refusing to assimilate is a form of knowledge as well. The refusal to be engulfed or erased by a dominant culture manifests itself with the movement of creative resistance and natural resilience that my grandfather Labib represented so well. For instance, he learned French during the French colonial mandate, but just enough to get by, not enough to have a deep conversation. The French language was regularly and collectively mocked and purposefully butchered by the Lebanese people as a way to discredit its superiority and render it too comical for any serious matter. Refusal disempowers the oppressor.

Our knowledge was kept through the women and the elders who were tasked with relaying the sacred knowledge from one generation to another. Certain information was kept secret or behind the mountain of shame, and it would only be revealed a few generations later as the secrets unfolded. But it was through the recipes that contained knowledge around harvest, around hygiene and beauty, around history and even fashion, that Indigenous and traditional knowledge was transmitted. This was the ancestral knowledge that taught us how to dye fabrics with plants, and how these same plants were medicinal, and how we could use them to heal our physical and psychic wounds. My grandfather learned all this from the women that surrounded him. Loved by many, he was a school in his own right.

My grandfather's learning journey, self-imposed discipline, and creative resilience provided a sort of compass for me personally. The radical learnings I encountered on my path are from my experiences and are far more intense than any knowledge I could have passively received in a classroom. Experience and know-how are the invisible PhDs we accumulate without the certification from colonial establishments. In Arabic we have a saying that essentially translates to "Don't trust the one who knows without having experience; trust the one who has experienced it and has found knowledge through practice." This is the ultimate permission to trust the learnings we gather simply by living our life.

The world is in a constant state of transformation. Jobs are no longer the ultimate goal, and a traditional career makes little to no sense in this time of chaos and climate change. What will a job that upholds and reinforces an extractive system of oppression help me accomplish in life? Our youth are questioning the very notion of professional careers, productivity, and workaholism that some believe are essential in creating a path forward.

In the case of my grandfather Labib, his creative spirit wanted him to explore engineering, but because he was taken out of school and forced to work at such a young age, it was extremely hard for him to gain the confidence and the tools, not to mention the funds, to excel in engineering classes. His path shifted as he began to teach himself architecture through materials, history, designing structures using metal, and understanding physics. His learning journey wasn't linear or conventional.

When he became a teenager, he was hired on a construction site. He worked long hours in the sun, and once he turned seventeen, he traveled to the Sahara to work and live there and learn how to build cities from sand. Le Corbusier and the brutalist movement clearly served as an inspiration to him in the way he juxtaposed concrete with glass and used marble in a nontraditional way. Grandfather Labib was able to rise from a small helper to an established worker and eventually to a self-taught master of architecture before he turned twenty years old. He worked on various projects building large and small structures, becoming better and better along the way.

The lesson I took from knowing his story was to allow life to transform me—the pain, rejections, and betrayal must be transmuted in order to design and follow a new direction forward. This can be applied to a personal path, a career choice, or to a more high-level initiative. For instance, in my case it proved to be the inspiration behind learning how to design adaptive systems to counter the effects of climate change, as well as how to limit the acceleration of climate change by creating new systems altogether that respond to stress points better than the systems currently in place. After all, a core concept in architecture is to calculate the stress limit of a given structure in order to prevent it from breaking.

After we left Montreal to return to Lebanon, when I was around thirteen years old, I was able to get to know Grandfather Labib in a much more profound and intimate way. He always encouraged me to draw, a gift I was born with just like he was. Drawing was my way of processing the world around me. In Montreal I drew cartoons and created comic strips, which I continued to do in Lebanon. I made fun of my teachers in these cartoon drawings and told stories that were important to me through illustrations. I doodled in the margins of every math notebook—creating caricatures of my mean math teacher or turning the zero I received in algebra into a portrait. I passionately wanted to pursue the arts, and it was Grandfather Labib who convinced my parents to allow me to attend a weekend art class.

On Saturdays I gathered my drawing paper, pencils, and painting kit and walked to my teacher's place. She was a French artist living in Beirut who was offering advanced art classes in her apartment. They were serious classes that often lasted longer than three hours and consisted of lessons in the classics: drawing live models and still lifes, learning perspective, shading, light, and depth, and practicing various techniques.

When we were introduced to the self-portrait, we talked about Frida Kahlo and how she proudly drew every single hair of her mustache and between her eyebrows (while we girls were plucking away at our facial hair, trying desperately to remove every sign of our ethnicity). Not only were we learning drawing and painting techniques, but we were learning about self-acceptance and natural beauty. My teacher also taught us art history. She wanted us to have all the necessary knowledge and skills to get into the top art schools in Paris, which had become a dream of mine.[7] My hope was to attend one of the public art schools in Paris because they were free and far more prestigious than the expensive private schools.

After art class I would go with my family to visit my grandparents. My aunties and cousins would be there already, the aunties equipped with their cigarettes, sipping coffee, ready for storytelling time. My grandfather was always the center of every gathering. He told us story after story about what it was like to live in Beirut during the war, his time working in the Sahara, and how he met my grandmother. I listened to the stories and drew in my sketch pad, inspired by the worlds I wished I'd known. I loved being around my grandfather; he affirmed my love for the arts and creativity. He knew what was real and needed in this world, and what was a complete waste of time. There wasn't anything that could impress him more than the vibrant creative energy of someone trying to create something new.

A few years after our arrival back in Beirut, I had

befriended two girls, Ana and Hala, who were, like me, deeply invested in the arts. Ana's Russian mother was excessively strict, carefully building her daughter's art career, and enforced a disciplined and focused approach to art making. She would make sure Ana spent her summers in Russia learning directly from the greatest living artists. My other good friend, Hala, was like me, self-taught for the most part.

Ana was enrolled in the local art school and encouraged me and Hala to join her. At first my parents were totally against my participation; the tuition was prohibitive, and they believed artists lived tortured lives. For them, following your passion to become an artist, even if you "made it," was completely unacceptable. Frivolous. Vulgar.

Who did I think I was to even think that way?

My parents thought I ought to find my way in the world by fitting into the capitalist structure, by obeying the laws of society, and by making an honest, decent living while also living a life of service to my family and community.

"The art world is not for people like us," said my father.

"You have to be reasonable, Céline, the arts are not a place for you," said my mother. "You're already half crazy. What are you going to do as an artist? Most artists lose their minds."

Their comments would enrage me, but I also understood what they meant. After all, we were living in a postapocalyptic world. There was no real place for the arts in their mind; that field of work was not reasonable. We weren't aristocrats whose livelihood was set. We had to figure out a way for ourselves to be able to make money and help our community. But something in me was relentless, and Grandfather Labib continued to encourage me to keep working on my art in spite of the fact that I wasn't allowed to go to the art school.

Ana's mother was the opposite of mine. She was the one who'd found the local art school and continually monitored the teachers there to make sure they were providing her daughter with the best possible education available in Beirut. Her goal was for her daughter to be an accomplished artist. Ana's technique was flawless; she mastered watercolor and oil painting like an experienced professional, yet she was only sixteen. After weeks of convincing my grandfather to talk to my parents on my behalf, I was finally allowed to go to the art school, and that was the beginning of a journey that eventually took me to Paris.

On August 18, 2001, my mother and I were sitting side by side in an airplane poised for departure. I was crying uncontrollably because even though this was my dream, I was leaving the love of my life behind in Beirut. As I looked to my mother for comfort, I noticed that she was also weeping.

Stunned, I asked, "Mama, why are you crying? You're going to return to Beirut after this week. I won't be!"

She looked at me, unable to utter a word.

I could not understand why she was crying more than I was. I wanted to be held and consoled by her. It didn't cross my mind that she was crying because I was leaving the nest. We were always fighting and famously never got along. I didn't know yet that when your firstborn leaves home it triggers an avalanche of emotions. It was as if the mountain of shame holding all emotions back had transformed into a volcano.

As the plane taxied down the runway and my mother melted with sadness, I held her hand tightly. Then we were aloft, flying out of Beirut International Airport on our way to Paris. The sacrifice parents make to get their kids the necessary, albeit colonial, education takes a toll on their bodies, their health, and their finances. Nonetheless, becoming educated is about opening up all roads, which inevitably leads to collective liberation.

NOTES

2. يا عيب الشوم is used to express that something or someone is shameful. It literally translates to "shame on the misfortune" (*shoum* means "misfortune" in Modern Standard Arabic).

3. The San Remo Resolution, passed on April 25, 1920, determined the allocation of Class "A" League of Nations mandates for the administration of three then-undefined Ottoman territories in the Middle East: "Palestine," "Syria," and "Mesopotamia." The boundaries of the three territories were "to be determined [at a later date] by the Principal Allied Powers," leaving the status of outlying areas such as Zor and Transjordan unclear.

4. Six of the first seven prime ministers of Lebanon were alumni of French schools, mainly the Jesuit schools, as stated in Esther Möller's chapter, "Elites as the Least Common Denominator: The Ambivalent Place of French Schools in Lebanon in the Process of Decolonization," in Jost Dülffer and Marc Frey's *Elites and Decolonization in the Twentieth Century*, Cambridge Imperial and Post-Colonial Studies Series, Palgrave Macmillan, London, 2011.

5. *Annals of the Caliphs' Kitchens*, written around the 10th century by Ibn Sayyār al-Warrāq, is the earliest-known medieval Middle Eastern cookbook. As Charles Perry writes in his foreword to

Medieval Cuisine of the Islamic World, "there are more cookbooks in Arabic from before 1400 than in the rest of the world's languages put together." *Annals of the Caliphs' Kitchens* wasn't translated into English until 2007—by Nawal Nasrallah (an Iraqi immigrant to the United States), who stumbled upon the book while doing research for her own Iraqi cookbook. It boasts 615 recipes pulled together from 20 different cookbooks and also contains a treasure trove of poems dedicated to culinary curiosities.

6. Charles al-Hayek, Lebanese historian.

7. Why was I drawn toward the capital of our colonizer? Here I am, raging against French colonialism and education and advocating going back to our roots and traditional knowledge, yet I actively chose to spend my most formative years there. This is exactly why I am writing this story. All our stories are rooted in contradiction. While those in the Global North would see this as hypocritical, we see it as a pull toward the belly of the beast. All our dreams are to leave our country at some point, and as we have been bombarded culturally by the North's culture, we are deeply drawn to it.

CHAPTER II

Of Sacred Rebellion & Joyful Defiance

Cassette #2: WhatsApp file

Oud playing, a familial gathering is being heard; it's my great uncle Tony playing for his sister Souad. She begins singing with a voice so deep حنونـه *melancholic, emotional, the voice of a goddess. She sings while Tony plays, the family sings the chorus with her. It's a familiar mouwal, song, rhythm. They are singing together.*

To paraphrase Maya Angelou:

You must know those who have paid for you to be here—your ancestors. So, when you know their names, speak their names.

And I am here to speak their names throughout this book and to remember the lessons.

The sacred rebellion always brewing in my spirit is there to keep me in love with life. For a very long time I was labeled a troublemaker, a rebel without a cause, an angry feminist, or just plain crazy. But sacred rebellion is in fact a divine gift, for it is grounded in infinite love. It is respectful irreverence; it is the ability and will to demonstrate courage in the face of naysayers, bullies, and anyone whose motive it is to oppress or deny your humanity. It is the attitude through which joyful defiance is enacted and through which change is made. It is the truest expression of the creative spirit, the spirit we are all made of and all have the right to express.

There is a sacred rebellion that lives inside the bodies of women in my family who have taught me everything I know. The rebellion is brewing and active and has a song of its own. It marches to the beat of the blood pumping through the veins, rising with every breath and expanding with every inhale and every exhale. When the heart rate accelerates, the sacred rebellion's chant becomes louder. When the breath turns into a scream, the sacred rebellion is armed and ready for the revolution. A revolution that begins in every cell of the body, transpiring into sweat, moving women into manifesting their will into the physical world.

The sacred rebellion has the power to command its will into existence. The women who have taught me everything I know have often done so without uttering a single word. Most of what I've learned comes through observation. The way to understand this sacred knowledge is by learning how to read and feel the room. An invisible stream of information exists where words are obsolete. This is why trying to describe this way of being by using words may dilute its very essence.

This is a form of knowledge and intelligence that cannot rely only on words but on the meaningful exchange of looks, the reading of facial expressions, the deep understanding of eye movements, or the feeling of touch that carries a clear direction. Sometimes only a breath says it all. The sharp awareness and attention it takes to read a swift movement, such as eyebrows that move up and down once while eyes are closed and mouth emits a "tsk" between barely open lips, constitutes a form of invisible knowledge acquired as a common skill in various cultures of the Global South. This information may translate to *You'll see what's gonna happen* or *I dare you.*

I dare you to access the Sacred Rebellion that lives in your heart and to allow that rebellion to move you toward Joyful Defiance! Defiance that creates change, that loves madly, that takes leaps into the unknown, that screams from the mountaintops, and that embraces personal power for the good of all.

My mother was carefully placing our suitcases against the door of our hotel room.

"What are you doing?" I asked her.

"I'm protecting us," she replied between sobs. The strongest woman in the world, my mother, was afraid.

"Paris is dangerous," she declared.

We lay down next to each other on a very small bed in a minuscule Parisian hotel room. My mother hadn't stopped crying since the plane departed Beirut. I'd decided to swallow my tears. I had to be the strong one. Our plans to secure a place for me to stay in Paris had fallen through. Either the rental was a scam or in a location deemed too dangerous. This was long before Facebook and Airbnb; all we had was word of mouth, which wasn't always reliable. Paris was, in fact, dangerous, far more than Beirut.

Before we left for Paris, friends and family had shared stories of being held at gunpoint or threatened with a knife in the Metro before being robbed while the Parisians walked past them as if they were invisible. Beirut was a lot safer. In Beirut, people looked after each other. There was a deep sense of community care and trust that could only be found in Indigenous communities and Black and immigrant neighborhoods in the Global North. In Paris, generally it was dog eat dog. Strangers would avoid you on the street, in the subway or anywhere else, especially if you appeared to be in distress.

Also, Paris was dirty. My mother was particularly shocked by the filth. French folks smoked in cafes, tapped their ash on the floor, and tossed their cigarette butts next to hundreds of others on the floors and sidewalks. My mother had never been to Paris before, and her conception of it was idealized. She was part of the generation of Lebanese who grew up under the shadow of the French Mandate and were forced to endure a strict French education. French colonialists portrayed themselves as more sophisticated, more modern, and more evolved than their Arab counterparts. And so, to witness the filth in front of her eyes enraged her. She even turned into a rebel, growing more confident in expressing her own identity, even though it was not advisable or particularly safe for her to demonstrate her Arab pride in Paris.

Part of our time together in Paris was spent dealing with the French authorities who were supposed to be helping us with my immigration paperwork. Sitting in endless waiting rooms together, we experienced countless instances of racist behavior toward us, which was obviously justified by the French belief that Arabs are the dirtiest form of human life. Black and Arab folks experience systemic oppression in France, sanctified by the French government. We also often experience legitimized violence as a result of the general acceptance of casual racism. There is a strong bond of solidarity between Black and Arab folks in France, being at the receiving end of the oppressive culture drawing from hundreds of years of extraction and control. Colonialism is not a thing of the past, it is a cultural, systemic, and economic reality that aims to universalize white European values and criminalize the "other."

On multiple occasions my identity was used as an insult. I heard the term "dirty Arabs" frequently, which offended and revolted me. The truth is that our people invented soap in 2800 BCE by upcycling the olive skins used to make olive oil and mixing them with ash, thousands of years before soapmaking finally became common in France only a few hundred years ago. Our people invented baths. During the Ottoman Empire, the bath houses in Tripoli, Lebanon, were famous and very popular. I'm not trying to romanticize my culture, but we pride ourselves on cleanliness and the appreciation of beauty through adornment. It is even part of our ancient religions. Long before the Abrahamic cults that imposed division amongst our people, water was considered both sacred and mystical. Bathing or cleaning oneself had spiritual significance long before the concept of baptism came into being.

In fact, the word "dirty" should be attributed to Europeans—specifically during the Middle Ages into the Renaissance—who were known for being so filthy that their own diseases decimated them. In fact, their diseases were their most effective weapons during their colonial forays into the Americas and Africa. To call our people dirty is not only historically and factually incorrect, it ignores the fact that humanity's collective survival depends on many inventions that came from Arab cultures.

Although my mother and I famously had never agreed on anything, somehow we began to find common ground in Paris through our observations. Before this trip, my mother was promoting the idea that modernity was a gift to our people brought to us by the kind hearts of the colonial empire. Her generation continues to believe this deep down. We, the children of this "lost generation," were given European names and speak French better than we speak Arabic. Most of us identify with the West much more than we identify with our own culture. Most of us resent our own people and deep down seek approval from prestigious Western institutions. Many of us suffer from an inferiority complex and the incessant need to prove ourselves to the white oppressor or appeal to the white gaze.

The lost generation turned against their own kind by buying into the illusion of assimilation. This phenomenon is seen throughout cultures and ethnicities who have survived colonization. When colonized people rebelled against their own culture and against their own people, they would end up giving their power to their colonizer and handing their sovereignty to the ruling class serving the empire. But for my generation, as we struggle to recover from wars, political instability, corruption, and economic hardship, our rebellion is directed against the oppressive values imposed on us and the power that authorized erasure of our ancestors and our culture. The sacred rebellion in our hearts makes itself heard in every moment, and it grows louder with each generation. My personal rebellion was to transgress the mountain of shame built to separate us from our own knowledge systems and culture, and to create a road between our past, present, and future so that we could, with great ease, learn from our ancestors and guide future generations.

The first thing we purchased when we arrived in Paris were international phone cards that, once scratched, showed a secret code allowing for cheap calls to Beirut. My mother phoned my dad as soon as she could and again melted into a pool of tears. My dad was always in problem-solving mode, and while listening to my mother describing our dire living situation, he remembered that he knew of a young man in his twenties whose fiancée lived alone in Paris and worked as a nurse. After a few calls back and forth, my father sent us the fiancée's number. She was already aware of our situation and invited us to visit her place when we called.

When we arrived at her small yet charming apartment, she disclosed that she had no friends in Paris and was rather lonely. She was enthusiastic about the idea of having me as her roommate for the school year. My room would be the living room, and my bed, the couch.

"I'll be fine here," I said out loud as she was giving us a tour.

She explained that she worked long hours at the hospital and was rarely home. I moved in with her at the end of that first week in Paris, before my mother returned to Beirut. I didn't know this woman at all and hoped we would get along well. I can joyfully jump into any given situation with the utmost trust that God will catch me. I was raised this way. And I have found throughout my life that although things never quite happen the way I'm expecting, approaching life with joyful defiance accelerates my chances of learning and keeps my heart open.

Before my mother's departure, we invited my father's cousin Rachel, who had been living in Paris for decades by then, to have an afternoon coffee ceremony with us. My mother cried almost the entire time. I could read an entire book in my mother's mannerisms, in the way she looked me up and down, saying with her eyes, *You better not mess this up because women like you don't get a second chance.* It wasn't a comforting stare. It was intended to reach the depth of my soul and plant a big seed of doubt there so it would somehow take care of me on her behalf. She looked at me in a way that clearly said, *You've got some nerve going this far. Let's see how far you go before you make a fool of yourself.*

Rachel consoled her, saying, "You've made a very courageous woman, and a fierce one. She's going to make you proud!"

The seed of doubt in my spirit grew stronger, asking, *Will you ever make her proud?*

These were my mother's gifts to me: *Doubt your ideas, and don't trust your instinct too much or you might end up crazy, dead, or murdered. Be careful and be reasonable.*

I have often asked myself if this type of child-rearing was meant to nurture or simply ridicule me. Is this a continuation of some colonial teacher ridiculing and despising the pupil, attempting to shame the wild Arabness out of her; or is it in some way meant for the best, for my own strength and well-being, teaching me by daring me to overcome something she knows I can beat?

It took me years to turn these seeds into meaningful food for my soul. I have explored the depths of my fear and have risen up to be stronger and sharper than ever. I don't blame my mother for planting these seeds; I'm sure these were seeds someone must have planted in her when she was young and that were simply passed down to me. I was the first woman in my entire family line to leave on her own to study art and give herself a chance to become what her soul and spirit were loudly guiding her to become. That, in and of itself, was a powerful rebellion.

I have learned to revere the sacred rebellion that leads to joyful defiance. I have learned to understand that the growth of generations comes from both tradition and rebellion, and the sacred dance they dance together.

TO HEAR THE SACRED REBELLION:

1. Sit or lie down so you are comfortable.
2. Make sure your legs and arms are uncrossed.
3. Close your eyes and feel yourself expanding with each breath.

You are safe right here and now.
Breathe in.
Breathe out.
Breathe in and hold.

Count to eight.
Breathe out, longer and longer.
You may yawn.

With your eyes closed, picture the ideas that make your heart joyful, your spirit excited.

Hear your sacred rebellion! It is the voice telling you that you deserve this feeling of joy, that you deserve to be fulfilled. This is the voice that says you are allowed. It is your divine right to be in ecstatic motion toward what makes your soul vibrate with love.

The only way to connect with the sacred rebellion is to have the ability and knowledge to transmute painful emotions of deceit, anger, rage, and sadness into powerful medicines to restore and inspire action in the physical world. It can also be observed as the process of turning an oppressive thought into radical permission. Sacred rebellion commands reverence. It is the essence of transformative energy and is capable of shifting the constraints and turbulences facing an entire generation into a new paradigm of possibilities.

In Paris, my heart felt immense with possibilities. I was always deeply aware of the immediacy of death and the miracle required to remain alive. I survived war and racism and returned to my ancestral home. I grew up to be eighteen years old and took the leap of faith to exist within my biggest dream: to be an artist. Although I didn't get into my school of choice, I still made it to Paris. I was living in the 13th arrondissement and was a few Metro stops away from the applied arts school I was admitted to, located in the 11th arrondissement.

When I was finally all by myself, my mother safely back in Beirut, I would sit on my couch-bed, open my sketchbook, and let the joyful rebellion move through my fingers all the way through my pencil and transform into stories and illustrations.

"Art is a guaranty of sanity," Louise Bourgeois wrote on a small piece of paper.

I bought a reproduction of her handwritten message printed on a postcard at the Centre Pompidou during a retrospective exhibition of her work. This sentence by Louise Bourgeois gave me permission to approach my art practice. I have collected, and continue to collect, such permissions to enact my sacred rebellion.

Before I left for Paris, my paternal grandmother, Souad, blessed my travels with her favorite saying: *nehna jenness-na dayan*, نحن جنسنا ضيان, which translates to "We are built strong and made to last." This saying embodies the belief, and therefore the spell, that whatever comes our way, we can defy with strength. Our body and spirit are made to last and therefore outlive any and all that may oppose us. She always reminded me of how strong I was because I was made with the same bones she and all our ancestors were, and because that lineage held us, we were unbreakable. Our kind is long-lasting and persistent.

She taught me to see that whatever confronts us is there to ignite in us the necessary strength for our spirits, because the sacred rebellion grows stronger when faced with opposing pressures, just like a muscle gets stronger lifting heavy weights while defying gravity. The sacred rebellion is a form of intelligence that grows against crushing tensions.

When Grandmother Souad turned fourteen, she met Noor— twenty-three at the time—and they fell madly in love. She was a unique young woman, with thick golden hair and blue eyes. She was gifted with a voice that would pierce through people's souls. When Noor asked to marry her, Souad's parents refused.

Souad responded, "Either I marry Noor, or I will go to the convent," which in Arabic sounds a lot more dramatic. For a young woman as beautiful and talented as she was, it sounded like she was choosing a death sentence as the alternative.

Marrying for love wasn't common at the time; most families still favored arranged marriages. Nonetheless, Souad and Noor were absolutely determined and married within the year.

When Souad was just fifteen she gave birth to her son. She and Noor and their baby boy moved into their very own home, a modest village apartment. Their time spent enjoying the intimacy of their small family was short-lived; soon after, Noor's mother, Shams, moved in with them. Shams had lost her husband, Noor Sr., when her son was born, so she felt entitled to impose herself on her son's family. This put intense strain on Souad—still basically a child—and the high standards Lebanese women were expected to uphold around raising a child and maintaining a home meant she was expected to be an adult before her time. Souad's honor, as a woman, wife, and mother, was tied to her ability to keep up these standards. And she had to learn the hard way, under the scrutiny of a stern matriarch who had become her permanent houseguest.

Shams was the archetypal mother-in-law who wanted to break Souad's spirit. Although she could confide in her mother and sisters about how hard it was to please her mother-in-law, Souad alone was the one who had to face Shams. And no matter how hard she worked, she couldn't get Shams to respect her. The pressure she felt from Shams's judgment fed Souad's latent defiant spirit, sharpening her power and strengthening her (secret for now) sacred rebellion. This rising inner defiance proved to Souad that she could and would survive her mother-in-law's scrutiny.

Shams wanted nothing more than to erase Souad completely, to discredit her and humiliate her in every way. Whenever Souad and Noor wanted to go on a drive in Noor's new Mercedes, Shams insisted on joining them. She demanded that she sit in the front seat with her son, forcing Souad to sit in the back with the children. Souad was "dethroned" in front of her own children, diminishing her status as the matriarch of the family.

Souad and Noor could only glance furtively at each other through the rearview mirror. A gesture that reminded Souad of the family legend about what happened when the two of them first met. Family mythology had it that when Noor's handsome emerald-green eyes locked on Souad's ocean-blue eyes, it awakened the waves and made the mountains tremble so they touched the sky. However, the drama in the car had nothing to do with trembling mountains. The seemingly unintimidating, small, round-bodied mother-in-law kept an eagle eye on Souad with a small compact mirror hidden in the palm of her hand, while Souad stared from the back seat into the rearview mirror at Noor who discreetly glanced back at Souad—a painting in and of itself.

Shams attempted to establish her domination over Souad every day and put her in her place whenever possible. Years later these stories traveled as my grandmother confided in my mother when she was newly married to my father. She assured my mother that she would never behave the way Shams did. My grandmother was always careful to make sure my mother felt like she was the queen of her own home. She had enough confidence in my mother to allow her, the younger woman, to take her son and lead the way. It really was about confidence and love; both translate as respect for others.

At sixteen years old, Souad started smoking cigarettes on the advice of an older friend who insisted that this would make her look older and more sophisticated. She was famous for lighting a new cigarette off the burning ashes of the previous one. Back-to-back, literally, holding the consumed cigarette in one hand and the new one in the other. She had become a dragon. Despite the cigarettes and the heels, and all her attempts to make herself appear more chic and mature, Souad always retained her innocence and allowed the purity of a childlike love to be the compass in her life.

As I lit my own cigarettes, I always thought of her. I loved cigarettes. It was cemented as part of my identity when I got into the Nouvelle Vague French movies and discovered the concept of the *femme-enfant* (woman-child). I embodied it so naturally. She wasn't sexualized like the Lolita archetype; she was an intellectual woman whose childlike defiance was kept intact. And in a way I felt that my grandmother Souad was the archetype of the *femme-enfant*. A young woman who was both an adult and a child.

I discovered the medicine of "Lebanese Blondes," a blend of golden-colored hashish coming from Lebanon and popular amongst my peers. We mixed it with the tobacco in our hand-rolled cigarettes. The medicine brought me back to myself. I was able to create without the seeds of doubt. It was as if the Lebanese Blonde were quelling the doubts within me.

I befriended a girl in my class who happened to be my neighbor in the 13th arrondissement. Both of us were typical femmes-enfants. At eighteen we looked like characters from a Jean-Luc Godard film if he were to include an Arab main character. Our days began at ten in the morning, meeting at the local café, where each of us ordered "un café, s'il-vous-plaît" while lighting up a cigarette. We drank our coffees with our large black portfolios slung over our shoulders.

The portfolios were as tall as we were, and everyone who saw us exclaimed, "Ah, les artistes!"

We finished our coffees and cigarettes, threw the butts on the floor along with the others, watched the waitress sweep them up from what was essentially a wall-to-wall ashtray, and then off we walked to the Metro.

Mon Cinéma 2001

My favorite class was *Créa*, short for *Créativité*—a class on conceptual art that was as much a lived experience of conceptual art itself as it was a study of the subject. Everything I learned in the class—the conceptual rigor, the theoretical framework for enacting the change I want to effect in the world—gave me my direction to create and forge the career I ultimately developed, extending far beyond painting and drawing, into the performing arts, technology, cyberarts, and ultimately to establish my organization, Slow Factory, creating community and climate solutions.

The class was taught by "Patrick André depuis 1966"—his artist name: "Patrick André since 1966." During the course of that class, he and I developed a unique friendship. He became my mentor, and we began meeting for coq au vin and wine and hours of philosophical conversation.

One exercise that Patrick André asked the members of the class to do was to keep a visual journal. Every day we created a page in our journals. We were to use any medium we felt expressed our lived experience. We painted, drew, created collages, and even included found objects like used condoms. These journals represented a living archive of our existence. In the middle of the school year and without warning, Patrick André took our journals and distributed them randomly to the class members. We were now to create a week's worth of art in someone else's journal.

We all protested and rebelled against his idea. He promptly and in an authoritarian way interrupted our childish behavior. French teachers know how to shut a class down; it's absolutely mesmerizing to experience. The room fell silent.

He said, "Art is generosity. Give yourself to someone else's journal the same way you would for yourself."

He made us all want to give. We wanted to be artists, and this was the best example of what art actually is: the ultimate act of giving. And giving was intimately linked with who I was as a person and what my people pride themselves to be. We took the journals home, and for a week, we created some of the best visual entries in those journals that did not belong to us.

Patrick André and I met every week outside the school. He often invited me to visit him at another French school where he was the artist in residence. There, he was working on a series of public art sculptures. While out walking one day, we passed by one of his sculpture series:

multiple replicas in slate of Snow White, each figure about twenty inches tall. They were so beautiful, yet most of them were vandalized. Students had written with chalk all over them and at times broken them entirely. Patrick André commented that art doesn't belong to us, and that he felt the way others had transformed the statues contributed to his art and created a new work.

This was the beginning of my interest in the concept of "touch the art" and interactive art installations. Patrick André told me that he had once, as a work of performance art, mailed all of his belongings, one at a time, to random names and addresses he found in the phone book. He got rid of everything he owned and was left sitting naked on the floor of his empty studio apartment. This was a radical act of generosity, a concept I explore in a later chapter. In this context, I was completely enamored with his style; he did everything with such integrity and seriousness. Yet his main motivation was to express humor and explore the absurd. I understood him deeply. And he knew that I appreciated and understood him, his work, and the concept of the "theater of the absurd," which explores the idea that to create art in a world that is seemingly falling apart is inherently absurd.

Patrick André was fascinated with how many passports I'd amassed, and how many languages I spoke, considering how young I was. I'd lived a relatively short, yet intense, life, and he wanted me to create something that reflected my unique life experience. He suggested I create an inventory of my formal government IDs as well as a list of my personal belongings. This assignment appealed to me because I was always interested in the idea of identity and home. Both were topics I desperately needed to explore on a personal level, having lived in the East and the West, and yet not knowing much about who I was.

Patrick André said to me, "Alors, fais ton Cinéma," which translates to "So, do your own cinema." In English it may not mean anything. However, in French the opposite sentence, *Ne fais pas ton cinéma*, means "Don't start acting out," "Don't start making up stories," or "Don't try to manipulate me." The positive inversion, *Fais ton cinéma*, is a sentence nobody would ever use. Patrick André gave me permission to embark on exploring and creating my personal mythology and to turn my lived experience into art.

I began working on a clapboard, the object that the film editor uses to find where the video and audio of each take are synchronized. I created the clapboard from foam board and carefully collaged black and white strips of paper, and the words "Mon Cinéma" on the foam clapboard. My artist name came to me at the same time as well: "celinecelines," because the second céline is plural—a play on the French grammar rule that determines what takes a random "s," and what is pronounced and what is silent. Patrick André didn't really like my artist name. He said it sounded like a stutter. But I liked that it was a stutter; it was just the stutter I felt I needed in order allow myself to wholeheartedly create.

It was joyful defiance to exist in Paris at that time, allowing myself to create. I had arrived in Paris shortly after
9/11, and the entire year was about what the Arab identity meant for the safety of the West, and what Arabs were
allowed to contribute, if anything at all. I began documenting my travels, filming from the airplane window as I flew
to Beirut for Christmas that same year. I arrived in Beirut,
and the warmth, humidity, and proximity of all the people
in the airport held me as I began to cry. I was home, home.
I was where I felt I belonged. With my clapboard at the
ready, I began filming a series of self-portraits. In these
self-portraits, I rolled an empty, large black suitcase around
Beirut. This was to represent the displacement stories of
so many like me who'd had to flee their homelands and
then later on were not able to return to live in their countries of origin.

There are millions of Lebanese people living around
the world, which, after decades of emigration, represents
a significant brain drain in Lebanon. When folks between
the ages of eighteen and forty leave their homeland in
search of work, safety, and opportunities elsewhere in
large enough numbers, they leave their home country
destitute. Without these young artists, scientists, and
entrepreneurs, there is little innovation and none of the
positive change and cultural and scientific advances that
come with innovation. In 2011 the Arab Spring brought
a significant number of us back to Lebanon with the desire to follow the famous folk song of postwar Lebanon:
"Raje3 Yet3amar Lebnan," راجع يتعمر لبنان, "Lebanon will

be Rebuilt." Our hope was to bring to our country, and therefore the region, innovation, technological access, and new life.

The year in Paris ended with me crying by the Seine on the phone with Patrick André, who was consoling me. I had not been given the right to move to the next year; the school I was in had recommended that I go into a conceptual art program as opposed to my current applied arts and design program. To them, I wasn't a "functional" artist, I was a "conceptual" artist who wasn't going to be a productive member of society as a graphic designer or a creative director. This was not the last time my imagination was dubbed too "radical," branded as too full of wild ideas to be practical or useful to traditional industries. Little did they (or I) know that some years later I would build a creative media empire in which art, design, science, and engineering would be used in an interconnected way to solve existential threats such as climate change.

After I left Paris, Patrick André and I continued to cocreate while I roamed around the world. Our correspondence kept me sane and provided me with an anchor through the motions of life. *L'art c'est la vie* (art is life) was my motto. Indeed. I made sure of it. Between 2001 and 2006 I continued to develop *Mon Cinéma*, exhibited my work in galleries, and was invited to create art and video for artists who were represented by the independent English record label, Ninja Tune. As I worked on *Mon Cinéma*, the self-portraits became less about me documenting myself as an ever-changing person, and more about me as I saw myself within the political context of the life I was navigating between Montreal and Beirut. My suitcase continued to remain front and center in my video portraits. The suitcase was a perfect representation not only of my lived experience, but of the experience my entire generation was having. So many of us were forced to flee, and eventually totally uprooted from our country, causing us to work abroad and send money back home.

On July 12, 2006, my suitcase was packed sitting on the floor of my Montreal apartment, ready to fly with me to Beirut, filled with vitamins, medicine, clothes, and beauty products that can only be found in North America. I had all the gifts wrapped for each of my cousins, aunties, mother, grandmothers, grandfather, father, sister, and brother. Expats always return home with suitcases filled with gifts. I'm not the only one who approaches the return with such sacred reverence. We plan in advance, at times even six months prior to the trip, to begin gathering gifts and goods to bring home. An entire closet is dedicated to storing these goods, slowly purchased throughout the year.

At five in the morning, my phone rang. It was my mother who was calling me from Beirut. All I heard was: "You're not coming to Beirut today, Israel bombed the airport." Then the line went dead.

I rose from bed in total panic, turned on the television to CNN's "Crisis in the Middle East." Their reporters were justifying the attack by claiming Israel had to defend itself from Lebanese terrorists. It made absolutely no sense. The images on the television were traumatizing. Many had died, and Israeli tanks were entering Lebanon. I placed a VHS tape in the machine and began recording the news while compulsively calling my mother's cell phone in Lebanon to no avail. No calls were going through, as is usually the case when major explosions happen. My sister was living with me in Montreal at the time, and she and I were in shock and tears the entire day as we saw our flight being canceled and watched our country being bombed on live television. We couldn't eat anything and smoked entire packs of cigarettes in tears between prayers and attempts to call my mother's cell phone.

Finally, at around 3:00 p.m. that day, we got through and heard my mother's voice saying "Don't worry! It's not as bad as it looks on TV." I hit record on my voice recording device, and she repeated, "Don't worry! There's nothing! It's not as bad as the news says it is!" Then the line cut again.

We had CNN on the television without interruption and weren't able to sleep at all that night. The news covered the "Crisis in the Middle East" for long stretches of time interrupted by long stretches of commercials. Our eyes were swollen and our lips dry from having smoked so many cigarettes while crying uncontrollably. Brian, my sort of boyfriend, finally came over to take us out to eat something.

The last thing we heard my mother say was, "Leave your suitcase by the door. They will rebuild the airport, and you will be able to fly here in a few days."

We held on to that thought; it kept us alive. Brian stayed over to keep an eye on us and make us laugh. He was particularly hilarious and made all sorts of inappropriate jokes. We weren't able to control ourselves from crying as we sat on the balcony howling. By morning I had four VHS tapes filled with CNN footage and had managed to record my mother's voice on cassette tapes. My goal was to overlay her voice on muted CNN footage of the 2006 war showing Israeli tanks invading Lebanon, bombing the airport, bombing our power plant, and devastating entire cities.

When my mother called us early in the morning, she kept repeating, "Don't worry! We are fine! Please stop crying! Be strong, you are the eldest, you have to get yourself together. There is nothing happening."

As she said these words, an explosion occurred on television, and we weren't able to even listen to her denying what was going on with a jovial voice. It was surreal. We hung up, smoked more cigarettes, cried some more, this time while sitting next to our suitcases. We didn't dare open them at all. We were convinced that what our mother said was going to happen. Of course, they would rebuild the airport and this nonsense war would end soon.

But the war didn't end that fast; in fact it was called "The July War." It lasted thirty-four days and took much longer for Lebanon to recover. The suitcases were left untouched. We used whatever was outside the suitcases, did our laundry often, and didn't open our suitcases to remove any item from them.

During this period I was pursuing a career in the arts. I had received a bachelor's in communications and cyber-arts and was considered for a master's program in cyberarts. My focus of research was the study of nature through technology, which never saw the light of day. During the 2006 war, I was confronted with an existential slap in the face. One night, sitting on the balcony smoking and crying, I heard my parents' voices say to me: *The art world is not for us! You need to find a real job and make a real career so you can take care of yourself and your family.*

All the pushback I had faced when I initially wanted to go to Paris became more real. I understood their point of view in a visceral way. My main worry was about helping my family exit Lebanon and come to Canada. A lot of international boats were leaving the Beirut port and taking Lebanese refugees to safety. Canada had a boat ready, and my parents were considering fleeing for the second time in their lives. If they were to come to Canada, I would need to help them in every way. And that wouldn't be possible with an artist's career and a master's in nature and technology.

I sent a letter to my program director and quit the master's program. I sat in front of my computer, opened Photoshop, and began creating a fake design portfolio. Ads for all sorts of products that were featured on CNN. Fake magazine covers and all kinds of typographic works with poetry I had written. Brian was also of the school of thought that art is for the rich, and if you really want to make it in this world, you need to turn your art into survival and work. He and I worked together on several projects, mainly video projects, and he was always very encouraging of my work. I'm agile with software and quick at conceptualizing and creating.

In the evening he would sit on the couch next to me as I completed my fake design portfolio and exclaim, "You're so talented! You're so good at this."

It made me feel so good to hear these words, especially coming from him because he was sort of a mentor to me. His creativity was sought after and he had been hired as a creative director even though all he was able to do was come up with out-of-this-world ideas, then folks like me would get inspired and make them happen. I loved him so much. He inspired me and gave me confidence in what I was capable of doing.

As soon as the portfolio was ready, he said, "My best friend is Lebanese, he has a design studio. You should work for him. He'll groom you to be a good designer, you have the base for it."

Brian arranged a time for me to meet with Ghaith, his Lebanese best friend. We met in a restaurant nearby, and I showed my work. We had a short interview, and I was hired as a junior designer. In the portfolio I included some graphic work I had done for Brian and various events. We were somewhere in the end of August by then. I came home, took a long shower, and cried a lot. It felt both amazing and scary to be in that place of hope and despair. CNN was still going on with the "Crisis in the

Middle East," and the VHS tapes were now piling up. I had close to a dozen sitting under the television.

My sister and I finally opened the suitcases. We pulled out every gift and returned them to the closet, safely tucked away for the next trip. We removed our good clothes and placed them in our drawers. We pulled out our shoes and favorite things, then closed our suitcases and placed them in storage. We called our parents once again to make sure they were safe. They had decided to stay in Beirut near our grandparents and to not abandon them at this stage in their lives. We were once again separated from one another, yet closer than ever. I shared the good news that I had taken on a new job. My parents were encouraging and ecstatic that I had somehow finally gotten some sense into me. It was like I had become an adult and now was blessed with the responsibility of holding my family and my community. I was making the right decisions and the right sacrifices in order to survive. Because art wasn't for us. We were made to work.

The last art piece I edited was the CNN footage with my mother's voice laid over the muted video. I spent days creating it. Editing every scene, every moment. Reliving the trauma and crying a lot more. I imagined that this could go into a gallery someday: *Broken Realities*. It turned out it was easy for me to learn new software and coding. I threw myself headfirst into the internet. At the time, the internet was viewed through a negative lens. All industries were being affected by the openness of the web and were slowly crumbling as their corrupt ways were being exposed. The internet was shining a light on the infrastructure and systems of every industry, starting with the music industry. It was the first to collapse since the web rendered the physical media of musical objects obsolete. The internet truly brought every industry to its knees and forced them to reimagine themselves with more ethics, more transparency, and a focus on the end user. I loved that era altogether and began designing systems, databases, information systems, and architectures. This was done with the mission of making information accessible in the most transparent and intuitive way possible.

When I shared my new experiences with Patrick André, he reminded me that what I was now doing was a form of art. L'art c'est la vie. It's how you approach it. It consoled me to hear this as I had consciously left the hopes of ever becoming an artist far away during the July War. My hopes and dreams blew up when the Beirut airport was bombed. To hear again that art is life gave me permission to handle each design project with the same respect I would have for an art project.

As I learned about interaction design, which is the task of designing interactions between the machine (the computer) and the end user (you), I started documenting my learnings in a blog online. I would share lessons learned and books to read to approach the topic from an architectural or a cultural perspective. We were encouraged to have a broad range of knowledge rather than a specific narrow point of view. Because the field was fairly young, we were all openly learning and sharing knowledge.

My blog garnered the attention of peers in the open knowledge community who introduced me to Creative Commons and the open licensing of art, music, books, and open libraries. The concept of accessibility and openness was extremely attractive to me. It was resonating with the idea that "art is generosity." Art is generosity, and so is the access to information, open libraries, and open knowledge. My world expanded, and with each open, free online learning tool, I became a better designer and a better writer. Soon I started teaching what I knew to others, misfits like me who'd found their place in the open web culture—a culture of its own. It was all about giving back to the community, contributing to the common good, and sharing knowledge. Ethics I hold dear to my heart.

Ethics came to me naturally through my family, my culture, the Indigenous teachings of the women in my life, as well as the value system of the Global South in general, where the sacred is an everyday lived experience. These ethics that I hold dear might at first glance seem contrary to the idea of sacred rebellion and joyful defiance but are actually the bedrock of those ideas. For without deep love, connection, the security and ritual of tradition, and the foundational belief in the value of education in all its forms, I would not have been brave enough to make the hard choices I did, to go against the flow, to dare to transform systems. I would not have been able to imag-

ine more for myself or been able to pivot, to make different choices, to experiment, to learn and unlearn and then
learn something new and keep going in that ever-ex-
panding spiral. I would not have been in a position to
give back to my community and step out into the world
with my joy intact in spite of the hardships I've experienced and the horrors I've witnessed.

CHAPTER III

Heal Your Mother's Mother

On Radical Care

Cassette #3: أنا الأم الحزينة
"Anal Oum el-7azina"

Fairuz sings "Anal Oum el-7azina," a hymn sung on Easter from Mother Mary's perspective after burying her own son, murdered at the hands of the colonial occupation of Palestine at the time, the Roman Empire; Jesus, Yassou3, a rebel, represented the resistance. Mother Mary laments his death through the voice of Fairuz; once Fairuz's version ends, my grandmother Souad's version begins, a rough recording with noise on the tape, her voice piercing through it. Tears run down my cheeks as I feel her voice in me.

On Radical Care

It has been said by Indigenous wisdom around the world—now finally being grudgingly proven by closed-minded Western science, as so much ancient wisdom is—that healing one's own wounds will heal back into the generations before. First, by healing your own emotional traumas and becoming more balanced and healthier, your behaviors can positively affect your relationships with living parents and grandparents. This healing can go further than the emotional level to the spiritual—what Western science can only understand in terms of "paradoxes" and now the evolving field of quantum mechanics. We shall see, in the years to come, the concepts once dismissed as "primitive superstition" be proven as true by science. All this is to say, there is more to healing than meets the eye, and healing our own relationships and wounds do have intergenerational effects. In this way we can see the wounds that have been imposed on our mothers and their mothers and see how they have been conditioned and imposed on by so much structural harm.

Often, it is women who are the first to impose oppressive structures on other women as they attempt to control their own and other women's bodies and minds. It is often women who dictate what is allowed for a woman to do and what isn't, a reflection of the oppression that has been forced upon them. When we choose to heal ourselves first, especially our relationship to power and control, we can break down the stone mountain of shame that resides in all of us, allowing for intergenerational healing.

The only way to heal our mother's mother is by becoming aware of what it is we are healing, and how we can stop perpetrating harm on one another. A woman can unwittingly become an extension of the oppressor. It is often through the control of women's bodies that the controlling colonial mindset persists across generations. When a colonial entity occupies a land, it always follows the original playbook of domination. Local and Indigenous men are killed or imprisoned, women are raped, spiritual artifacts are burned, and Indigenous and native languages are forbidden. There is an instant criminalization of native identity that is perpetuated by the women in proximity to power. Their own survival depends on their obedience and enthusiastic perpetration of the crimes of erasure and oppression.

This is an effective way to control the next generation, whose lineage often contains the oppressors' blood. New generations are often less likely to rebel against their rulers if their education, their blood, their language, and their mothers are all telling the same story. It's a way to pacify the native people and rule relatively peacefully over new lands. Peace doesn't mean justice; it means stability and control. When we call for peace without justice, we often bury the wounds in the bodies of women and expect life to resume without much rebellion. But the rebellion never fades. It lives in the soul of every woman. A sacred rebellion. However, proximity to power may quiet down that rebellion. It may be bartered for safety and power. Women who find themselves in positions of power under patriarchy as trusted matriarchs often represent a form of control by proxy, a sort of policing imposed not by the patriarch in power but by its subordinates. Women policing women.

I was thirteen when we moved back to Lebanon in 1996. I was abruptly uprooted from my life in Montreal and separated from my interests and activities. I had been dancing and doing gymnastics since I was five, but in the Lebanon we returned to—postwar, postapocalyptic to me—there were few activities for children, and no dance or gymnastics classes for me to attend. After-school was often spent at my grandparent's or neighbor's home reading, playing backgammon, and listening to the adults talking about politics. I was deeply depressed during the first years back in Lebanon. Overhearing dreadful stories of rape, forced marriages, and the women who never married and committed suicide as a result, were terrifying for me. My future was bleak, and it seemed marriage was going to be imposed on me whether I was ready for it or not.

I began drowning my depression with food. I binged on sweets, which took me to a peaceful place for the few seconds they were melting in my mouth. The first summer in Lebanon I gained ten kilos (25 pounds), to my mother's horror. I was fat shamed and forced to be on strict diets that required eating only onion soup or salad or simply fasting. I broke the diets, secretly sneaking into the kitchen and stuffing my face with bread, cookies, and fruits. I knew that the bigger my body got, the less desirable I'd be. I was pushing the possibility of sex and marriage away from me. I refused to be the perfect Lebanese girl who was a size zero with long straightened hair and a hairless, perfectly brown body. I was big and curvy with my belly making multiple rolls before it hit my thighs. I replaced water with juice and gained a few more pounds. I camped out in the kitchen next to my grandmother and ate everything I could get my hands on. My mother and aunties were horrified by my weight and the ways in which I was, according to them, uglifying myself. I was shamed day and night for my fat body.

I responded to their criticism. "I love my body like this, I'm beautiful. One day there's going to be a celebration of fat bodies everywhere and people will worship curvy women."

My aunties laughed and told me I was crazy, that there would never be a day when curvy women would be acceptable. Yet here we are, we have seen this happen. But back then it was considered terrible and unsightly. My mother and aunties took it upon themselves to make me slim down by purchasing clothes that were too small for me to wear. They watched me jiggle and sweat trying to get into the too small pants or skirts, and then my mother would say with cruel satisfaction, "This is the size you're supposed to fit into. They don't make bigger sizes."

What was I supposed to do? Be the perfect Lebanese girl and be invited to make a family and live a small insignificant life? Or be big and break the curse of being an Arab woman? I chose to eat. I had a vision of women being celebrated in fashion for their beautiful and unique curves, and I was convinced that, one day, that would be me.

In art class with my teacher, a gorgeous round woman, I learned about the different body types celebrated throughout art history. We analyzed women's bodies and explored what history made of them as they grew fatter or thinner, depending on the fashion of the time. She encouraged us to model naked in class, and I happily volunteered to be the first to undress in front of my friends and model for them. I was probably a size 12 or 14 at fourteen years old when I started smoking cigarettes. The more I smoked, the less I ate. I began replacing food with the cigarettes I secretly smoked out on our balcony. I lost ten kilos (25 pounds) between the age of fifteen and sixteen yet continued to be considered fat by Lebanese standards.

It is common in Lebanon for women to make harsh comments about your appearance under the guise of being helpful. It is "for your own good" to know what people are saying behind your back. Comments are often delivered after making a loud inhale or "heeeee" sound to express mock surprise, as in, "Heeeee ... you've gained so much weight!" Or, "Heeeee ... your dress makes you look so fat!" Or, "Heeeee ... your hair looks terrible!" Or, "Heeeee ... your makeup makes you look old."

Women often hold grudges against each other. I have experienced this firsthand from women I have intimately known. I am discerning when meeting women who proclaim their love for me, as this love can quickly turn to control and jealousy. This is a result of patriarchal rule, and it's the main focus of healing our mother's mother because without acknowledging the grudge and bitterness women carry down their lineage due to pain, injustice, and suffering, it is practically impossible to reckon with healing these wounds. Women in my family would impose such rules on each other and on their friends, and vice versa. They expected the same behavior from women in their close circle.

As we divorce ourselves from patriarchal rules, we pick and choose the traditions we want to continue to uphold. And with that comes the loss of the thread of continuity between the past, present, and future. We are now, in a way, the detribalized, uprooted, multicultural mishmash of post-colonial reality trying to understand who we are and where we belong.

Good things came for me personally after the July War. I had the new position as a junior designer and weekend gigs working as a VJ (video DJ)—weaving moving images with sound and telling stories through joy and movement. Working primarily with found footage, I often used vintage films familiar to me from my childhood in both Lebanon and Montreal. I also used clips from Egyptian and Bollywood movies I'd watched as a teen in Lebanon and included special effects I designed. Creativity was loud within me. It poured out of me with ease in whatever medium I was invited to play with. Working with video made me feel like I was weaving stories and knitting a reality I could cope with.

I continued to edit the CNN videos I'd recorded on VHS as a way for me to make sense of nonsense wars. It was coming along, but somehow it became more and more emotionally difficult for me to open the files and reimmerse myself in the footage. Eventually I archived everything on an external hard drive to finish it at a later time—a time that never came because the hard drive broke and all my data was lost. This was very common in the days of backing up work on external hard drives before the cloud existed. Hard drives would fail often, and I have experienced the loss of information and my original works on multiple occasions from multiple hard drives.

Throughout my life the loss of artifacts and information has been a recurring theme. I was born in a war and experienced the loss of our home along with the artifacts in it: photographs, letters, art, clothing, jewelry, and cameras. And with every move out of a home and into a new one, across the ocean and back again, personal artifacts would be left behind, lost in a box somewhere unknown. Where would these memories go? I stopped holding onto them and accepted the generous absurdity that life presented to me. What comes will eventually go. And for that we have only the moment we are conscious of—the present. The past will soon disappear. The future doesn't exist.

It was winter before we were finally able to travel to Beirut—the airport now repaired and rebuilt as my mother promised. We packed our suitcases again with the same gifts from the previous summer. I took my small video camera to document what had happened to Beirut during the July War. Before the advent of iPhone cameras, I often brought my video camera along wherever I went.

I stood behind the tripod, looking through the eyepiece of my digital video camera, surveying the debris on the dusty street: a shoe, a decapitated doll, an open book with missing pages, a piece of newspaper, a pillow ripped open by a bomb, a burnt frame with no art or photo inside. Artifacts scattered on the ground with untold stories attached to them, like lost souls waiting to be heard. Lives interrupted as they were going about their day, violently silenced and erased. I stood there looking at the objects and holding the untold stories in my heart; it filled me with tears. I didn't know the details of these stories, I didn't know the names of the people who were attached to the objects, I didn't know their dreams. But I felt their magnitude.

The sense of loss I felt was palpable in the air. The sheer scale of destruction was an atrocity, but the flavor of the feeling of loss was familiar to me, a theme for my entire life. Loss of artifacts, information, memories, places, and homes have become just a part of the journey of life for me.

In late 2006 I was in the Dahiyeh neighborhood of Beirut, where the Israeli bombing just a few short months ago had been the most severe. It was dangerous to even be there and particularly dangerous to document the street life in that neighborhood.

Among my ongoing creative pursuits was filming an open-ended documentary with no defined purpose. I collected interviews with various interesting subjects, and shot landscapes and everyday scenes that moved me. When I was finally able to return to Beirut, I immediately went to the areas that Israel had bombed. I wanted to be in the middle of it. I positioned my camera on a tripod and spent an entire day filming from that one spot. This single uninterrupted shot exposed nothing and everything that was happening amidst destroyed buildings and shattered lives.

I had no specific purpose but to record one neighborhood that had survived the terror of the recent war. It was particularly dangerous because of the possibility of accidentally tripping over unexploded ordnances, and overall, because a camera on a tripod doesn't inspire ease in the traumatized population around me. The neighborhood is overwhelmingly populated by descendants of refugees from the 1948 Nakba, when Euro-Russian Zionist militia forcibly expelled 750,000 native Palestinians from their ancestral homelands to the surrounding countries such as Lebanon. The generations since have no citizenship of any country, few rights, and often limited legality to even work, with the Right of Return one of their only long-term hopes. It is within this grim reality that groups like Hezbollah emerged as alternatives to the often complete absence of governmental services available to displaced Palestinians. I'd had to receive permission from the local Hezbollah leaders to film there. We went to the checkpoint at the entrance to the neighborhood and discussed my ideas with the soldiers there. It was a frank, simple discussion explaining my project—very human and person-to-person in contrast to the types of bureaucratic interactions one has with government or security personnel in the West—and in short order we had a small paper authorizing our presence for the day.

The long-term violence and destruction resulting from the creation of the state of Israel in Palestine is still being felt across the entire region. The very existence of the "enemies" of Israel are entirely due to the fundamentally colonial nature of the Zionist project. For the now millions of intergenerational Palestinian refugees who survived the massacres and forced displacements beginning in 1948, watching the ongoing genocide and forced migrations, murders, kidnappings, and land thefts of their relatives and people across the border in Palestine that they cannot cross, must be so painful, day after day, year after year, decade after decade. And when certain factions turn to armed resistance, launching missiles across the

Blue Line, the "retaliation" is often extreme. "Mowing the lawn" is a military strategy whereby Israel periodically destroys civilian infrastructure, which prevents access to water and electricity, and poisons the water and landscape, including fields and crops.

Mainstream narratives around the July War in 2006 often begin with Hezbollah ambushing an Israeli military outpost, but without the context that the small piece of land in question, Shebaa Farms, was clearly a historical part of Lebanon. It was treated as part of the Syrian Golan when Israel invaded in 1967 and has been occupied illegally by Israel ever since. The killing of three Israeli soldiers by Hezbollah as part of this decades-old occupation became the excuse to blockade the entire coast of Lebanon, bomb Beirut and south Lebanon, kill thousands of civilians, and displace one million people.

To see it all now, in the trash-strewn street before me, I was overpowered by feelings of desolation, rage, and pain at the injustice of it all. The scene engendered such a profound sense of hopelessness. Yet I was deeply affected by the warm breeze and the sunlight that touched every surface; it was as if God were consecrating the entire neighborhood and all of Lebanon. The presence of God, Spirit, the Universe, was palpable. I was raised knowing that the supernatural is normal.

When the sun set, I pulled my equipment together and loaded it into my friend Hady's car. He had been instrumental in getting me access to that neighborhood and often acted as my "chaperone" while on expeditions in

Lebanon. Hady and I had many adventures in Beirut throughout the years. He was always my unofficial guide and protector, as I pointed my video camera at everything, literally everything I could capture. I was always trying to encapsulate what I had missed. Trying to save what will be lost. I have hundreds of tapes of Lebanon. I am always trying to absorb it as it absorbs me. I care deeply about my country and my people.

I met Hady when I lived in Lebanon as a teenager. He was my private math tutor; I had fallen behind at school and was desperately trying to catch up to the level of knowledge that is required in Lebanese schools. After having attended the Lycée Français in Montreal, I was behind in math, science, and Arabic. In Lebanon I received a rigorous education. Most educated Lebanese people end up speaking multiple languages from the get-go. Hady was a strict tutor and never laughed at my jokes. Nevertheless, I persisted. And he eventually became one of my closest friends. Through him I learned that I deeply hated math, but I also learned how to drive like a real Lebanese.

Hady was a miracle child in that he'd lived through a series of disastrous events that would have likely made anyone else's life unbearable. But his world view was sharpened by his lived experience. I was so drawn to his strength and knowledge of the world. Wisdom and knowledge gleaned from lived experiences are often discredited in the eyes and metrics of white supremacist models of success. Hady's survival had depended on the radical care of strangers, of an entire community that guided him throughout the years, overwhelmingly the women of the community. His story is not mine to share, as he told it to me in full confidence, and it will remain in a sacred place. But what I *can* share is that it has shown me the difference between the systems of radical care that exist in cultures of the Global South and what suffices for care in the Global North. Because we don't have the support of institutionalized care aside from private hospitals, most care is administered by our community. There's an Arabic expression that roughly translates to "Our community embraces and holds us." The way it sounds in Arabic makes you feel as if an entire family is hugging you.

Every time I go back to Beirut, I sit in coffee ceremonies and absorb stories I've never heard before. My maternal grandfather's mother, Grandfather Labib's mother, was a child bride who abandoned her still very young first-born child—Labib—and much older husband to run away with someone she'd fallen deeply in love with. This unforgivable act meant that she was shunned from her sisterhood circles, that she was without community. Her story was wrapped with the shame and judgment necessary to discourage any other women from that community from following her heart. What if she'd been held by her sisters? Maybe she would have been able to take her child with her. Maybe, if she'd been respected as a sacred being in the first place, she would not have been married off as a child. Maybe, if she'd been protected and surrounded by true love and friendship, she would not have had to abandon her child.

I've already described my paternal grandmother, Souad, and how her mother-in-law acted as her personal policewoman, scrutinizing her every move and making sure she never felt the necessary safety to expand and spread her wings. She was caged by this older woman who upheld patriarchal norms by wrapping Souad in shame and controlling her with abuse. Her mother-in-law dishonored and desecrated the very essence of her womanhood. A woman can go either way; we can oppress each other and grow the wall of shame that separates us from our essence, or we can break the walls down, and by healing our ourselves, heal our mother's mother.

Our sacred teachings are discredited and intentionally vilified by those who have colonized our lands. Colonialism has made sure to lock our Indigenous culture behind that wall of shame. Colonialism has gaslit us into believing that what we know has no value within the structures of modernism that it has erected on stolen lands and with stolen resources. Colonialism has left us with a legacy of doubt, uncertain if what we know and how we do things actually matters. But every day our stories find their way back to us. Because these stories are the truth, and they cannot be erased—like the fact that every single breath that has ever been taken on this planet is still here. From the extinct dinosaurs to the Goddess Ishtar and the legendary Cleopatra, their breath is the same breath we breathe.

My great-grandmother Mariam was a matriarch whose presence remains strong in my lineage. She took great comfort in knowing that she was breathing the same breath as Mariam Magdalena (in Lebanon we refer to Mary as Mariam), Mariam the Mother, and Jesus. She was a devoted religious sister of the Maronite Church from the time she was a young girl. She saw nothing but the supernatural, connected deeply with nature, and spent her time in devotion to God. As a young woman she was selected by the French colonial Catholic church to emigrate to France and serve God in a French convent. She was sent along with other Lebanese sisters, and with that opportunity she was awarded access to knowledge beyond languages and theology; she studied horticulture, geography, history, and literature among other subjects she was drawn to. This was the ultimate haven for her. Her deepest desire to be married to God was fulfilled.

Everything fell into place—except that she had suffered from a lifetime of acute migraines that forced her to stay in bed, in the dark, experiencing near-seizures each time anyone would visit her. At the convent she was often bedridden and forced to remove her nun's habit in order to wrap her head tightly in a scarf to relieve the pain of the migraine until it passed completely. (In the early 1900s migraines weren't even defined as such,[8] and this head-binding treatment was all that was available in France at that time.)

While living in Lebanon as a young girl, my great-grandmother used cupping therapy to relieve the pain of the migraines. Cupping therapy is a form of medicine in which suction is created on the skin with the application of heated cups. Its practice mainly occurs in Asia but also in Eastern Europe, the Middle East, and Latin America. If you were to Google "cupping" and land on Wikipedia, it would sadly discredit its benefits: "Cupping has been characterized as a pseudoscience and its practice as quackery." This is certainly a clear example of ancient Indigenous knowledge that has been purposefully discredited. Mariam would also use warm compresses soaked in water to which lavender oil, coriander seeds, and rose water were added. (In Middle Eastern and Asian cultures we believe that the cold enters the body and causes imbalance.) She would apply the warm, fragrant compress directly to her forehead. I learned to use these techniques myself as I have suffered from chronic migraines since I was seven years old. At the French convent, however, the medicinal plants she needed that are native to Lebanon weren't readily available, and cupping wasn't an acceptable practice.

As a consequence of not having access to the various treatments she'd used in Lebanon, Mariam would suffer in her dark room, missing days of service. Finally, the archbishop and mother superior of the convent decided to relieve her of her position as a sister. She was dismissed. Mariam, who was then in her mid-twenties and unmarried, was now considered an "old maid." Being rejected from the convent because of her chronic pain was devastating. She left the convent on foot, then took a train to Marseille where she boarded a boat to Beirut. In her suitcase were modest items of clothing, and around her wrist her wooden rosary wrapped between her thumb and index finger. Before she reached Lebanon, a letter with the news of her dismissal, which was delivered by an emissary of the convent, had already arrived at her parents' home.

Her dismissal from the convent and her status as an old maid brought tremendous shame to her family, so upon her return she was informed of her arranged marriage to a certain Sulaiman whom her mother had identified as suitable for her. Sulaiman was nineteen years old and mainly interested in chasing girls, playing cards, and running around with his friends. A small mustache was drawn close to his lips, his straight hair was perfectly waxed and combed back. He was handsome but vain, superficial, and immature. He managed to stay that way his entire life.

Mariam was well educated (much better educated than her husband), fluent in several languages, and had skills and interests far beyond the expected chores of a wife. Nonetheless, she quickly made peace with her life outside the house of God, realizing that the convent and the Catholic Church itself weren't big enough to contain God's spirit. Being rejected by the convent opened her eyes to God's presence outside the convent. She turned her devotion to her husband Sulaiman, a devotion that was comparable to her love for Jesus. The supernatural was natural to her, and that was how she raised her children, her children's children, and me, her first great-grand-child. Perhaps the way she made sense of her new path as a wife and mother was to surrender to whatever God's dream was for her. That dream would be lived with the same reverence as a life lived cloistered in a convent.

Great-grandmother Mariam was called Téta Marie (*téta* means "grandmother" in Arabic), and she was regarded as our family saint. The ways in which she communed with the divine through every aspect of her daily life confirmed her sainthood. She regarded her world as the convent, the world was God's creation and therefore worthy to be worshiped as is. She understood that the barrier we create between the world and the institutions we believe embody faith and culture is an imaginary border upheld by imagination and the illusion of control. When we realize that these boundaries are man-made and that in reality the world is far larger than the maze created by men, we can see that what holds us back is nothing but an illusion.

When I was older, long after Téta Marie had passed, I learned that her spirit was close to me when a fortune teller in New York told me that my great-grandmother on my mother's side would like me to know that she was right next to me and would be throughout my life. Tears ran down my cheeks as I felt the truth of this statement. My entire body heated up as her spirit embraced me. This is what I mean when I say that the cultures in most of the Global South live with Indigenous beliefs that understand spirits and magic and accept everyday miracles that are purposefully discredited, shamed, and considered a scam by the white man who could see but refuses to acknowledge the existence of the supernatural as it is impossible to control, dissect, and dominate. Spirits will not be controlled. And our spirits are the same. We cannot be subjugated; our spirits are free. When we acknowledge this, we begin to open up and heal. As we heal ourselves, we heal our mother's mother, and our lineage releases its tensions and is freed. It is popularly believed that what we discredit loses its powers. But in reality it just loses our attention and focus, it never really loses power.

If I close my eyes, I can smell Téta Marie's rice as it steams on her stove, cooking in a slow, traditional process. I smell her herbs drying in the sun and the aroma of gardenias in her garden. I see her silver hair pulled into a bun, the kitchen bathed in light, and the unexpected visitors coming in for coffee. Neighbors would make a circle with their chairs in the garden and sit with their coffee during our traditional coffee ceremonies. They loved to gossip and reveled in informing Mariam of what she already knew: that Sulaiman was cheating on her with a new neighbor.

Her grandchildren, including my mother, lived with Mariam when their mother left them there for months at a time. The girls always conspired to shock the uptight neighbors by hiking up their skirts and parading around in front of them, inciting a cascade of disapproving remarks and raised eyebrows.

"Mariam's grandchildren are street children!" they would exclaim.

Mariam laughed until tears came to her eyes at the

parade of underwear that was creating such chaos and disapproval among the neighborhood ladies. It was hard to know whether the ladies were more offended by Sulaiman's infidelities or the vulgarity of Mariam's granddaughters.

I have managed to collect these stories from years of interviewing family and friends whenever my schedule allows. I have asked my mother and her sisters to remember and recount the times they spent with Mariam. In the beginning, the wall of shame seemed completely impenetrable. I would get yelled at and told to stop asking questions. I have gathered and archived what I could collect of family photos, newspaper clippings involving my family, as well as any and all videotapes or cassettes tapes I could find. Family members would periodically send me audio files of my grandmother Souad singing in church, or of her brother Tony playing the oud. Every visit to Lebanon became a mission to collect, absorb, and record as much as I could from conversations, coffee ceremonies, confessions, and stories told about everyone and everything.

I am the exception. Most of the women in my family did not keep track of family memorabilia. They kept stories hidden from children and from each other, and whenever possible they would toss in the garbage any old energy they deemed ready to be given back to the world. It has been challenging to find anything predating my great-grandmother's time. Everything had been destroyed by war or thrown away with the goal of keeping the house uncluttered. We lived in minimal spaces before Marie

Kondo made it popular. Everything that existed in our home was there for a purpose. In my family, there was a general attitude of detachment toward objects and belongings. Money was hidden here and there in case we might need it. Instability and living in survival mode outlived the years of war.

We lived on borrowed time with stolen childhoods and the need to prepare each other for the worst. Asking my mother, her sisters, or my grandmother about the past was like touching a bruise and getting a reaction that was both defensive and angry. Through years of patient inquiry, I gained their trust and allowed them to be vulnerable and open up to me. Their stories eventually allowed me to understand why and how their lives ended up this way. Whenever I was able to spread my wings, it was done in defiance of their disapproval. And it wasn't because they didn't want me to be successful and happy. It was because they hadn't had the opportunities I've had. They barely experienced real childhood, sacrificed their dreams, and suffered in silence in ways I will never comprehend. Their bitterness, anger, and jealousy are rooted in their pain and hidden behind that wall of shame, forever remaining there. On a recent trip to Lebanon, I visited our Indigenous temples, the ruins that remain. The Romans pillaged our ancient villages and mostly demolished our places of worship and replaced them with their temples. Our ancestors managed to preserve some of these ancient locations by allowing the Romans to build their temples over the original temples. That way they were able to keep their temples and culture and sacred sites intact to a certain degree. These partly destroyed sacred places would remain secret places of worship for the Indigenous people of the land.

In the temples I visited in the Akkar region, there are intact stone sculptures of weeping women. Women who cried over the death of their lovers and infants, or the wrath of the gods who had destroyed their harvests, their villages, or their livelihoods. I was deeply moved by these 8,000-year-old statues, and how their tears still seemed fresh for the unknown losses they grieved. Fresh like the debris on that street in Dahiyeh so soon after the bombs punished the civilians of the neighborhood for daring to maintain a spirit of resistance to the colonial state that expelled their families from ancestral homes; fresh like my memories—still to this day—of the fear I felt when I realized I was less than twenty-four hours from arriving at the Beirut airport when it was bombed; fresh like Téta Marie's gardenias as she cooked her rice.

But the statues were also faded, like my memories of all those lost things I once kept in boxes that have long since disappeared; faded like the shame I felt when my classmates laughed at me, eroded by my years of healing and gaining pride in myself no matter my shape; faded, but not forgotten, like the Old Gods whose shrines still exist under the Roman and then Christian temples, whose names are still known and whose stories are still told.

One of the sacrifices many women in my lineage have endured is becoming a caregiver during childhood. In

Lebanese tradition, young girls are groomed to become caregivers to everyone around them: their siblings, their mother, and their grandparents. Childhood is prematurely terminated while grandmothers and grandfathers are infantilized, their autonomy stripped away from them and put in the hands of the children who care for them. My great-grandmother was cared for by the grandchildren who assisted her in every way. My mother was the eldest and Mariam's right hand. The unexpected advantage of this care was that she was allowed to stay up late when everyone else was asleep and was invited to spend time at night alone with Mariam watching Egyptian films. My mother's strength is in the wound of the responsibility and burden she was expected to hold at a very young age. Before she turned ten, she became responsible not only for herself but for the four other children her mother left in her care. This form of education isn't ideal but necessary for our survival. It is passed down from one generation to another. I too was expected to take on the burden of responsibility and raise my siblings.

At seven years old I became a proxy for my mother and was put in charge of my two siblings. On my own, I took care of them and made sure they were safe; I fed them whatever my mother cooked and entertained them. I invented games and told them stories, but I also held them accountable and was their source of comfort when they cried. In truth, I was too young to be responsible for them; I needed the same kind of care they were getting from me. The over responsibilities that came with this reality had repercussions into adulthood. I eventually required psychological healing, or as I think of it, rewiring, in order to balance out what was denied me in having such a short-lived childhood that was further interrupted by war.

However, there are also a lot of positive insights, and a certain level of fearlessness and resilience, to be gained by having grown up this way. To be able to survive alone with younger siblings, I had to reckon with fear and quickly learn to listen to my own judgment without letting fear take over. That skill alone is worth the experience of becoming a mother by proxy. The survival instinct it fostered has served me in the long run. Fear became a familiar energy that prepared me for danger. Once we can identify what danger fear is trying to expose, we can better prepare for it while remaining in charge of the situation.

Other lessons revolved around conflict resolution and deep listening. When children are raising children, they fight, and it can become very dangerous very quickly. Conflicts are sparked within seconds and can escalate into physical altercations if the person in charge doesn't find a safe and creative way to resolve the issue. In so many cases the sibling in charge may join the physical fight—again, a possibly dangerous situation. However, the positive takeaways from having to be in charge at such a young age are that powerful life skills become instinctual. Learning to listen deeply and compassionately and to ask open-ended, nonjudgmental questions are skills born of the need to restore harmony. Knowing what questions to ask and having the confidence to interrupt a quarrel to restore order are skills that cannot be taught through theory. These are skills learned through necessity and practice.

In mothering my siblings, I learned how to lead and navigate corporate hierarchies. An important part of leadership is the understanding of what to share with authority figures and what to keep hidden from them. Trust depends on integrity. The information that is meant to stay between siblings is sacred and cannot, under any circumstance, be shared with adults unless the adults can be trusted with said information. A trustworthy leader knows when to withhold information from those in positions of authority, thereby creating solidarity through true community care.

This approach is quite honestly the opposite of policing and delegating justice to a commanding authority. On the one hand, the adult will not be able to adequately know what to do with this information, and on the other hand, the child in charge often wants to protect the parent from over-worrying, or worse, to protect themselves and potentially their siblings from physical harm done by the parent. There is a level of inverse parenting that exists between the child who is sharing the responsibilities of mothering and the parent who is supposed to be mother/father. This form of caregiving is definitely less than ideal from the colonial sense of perfection, but it is way too often a necessity for women and children in the Global South.

So, instead of discrediting this kind of caregiving—born of tradition as well as economic necessity—or stripping it of its wisdom, I'm centering it and according it much-deserved respect. This respect allows us to explore it and understand the fruits it bears as well as the damage it does and how that damage can be healed. The healing of our mothers' mothers depends on how we work toward healing ourselves. Children can be extremely selfless when faced with challenges that threaten the survival of their families and communities. This selflessness can create misunderstandings later in life that must be unlearned at some point. For instance, we often find that there is a need to learn to mother ourselves to make up for the years we became mothers too soon. We may also find that we must attend to and nurture the child within who didn't have time to play.

One of the positive aspects of mothering my siblings is that I learned to cook. I carefully observed my mother, who takes pride in her cooking and is known for it. I loved watching her and my grandmother cook; they often cooked together while preparing our multicourse Sunday meals. They were both known for their traditional dishes, but my mother also experimented with fusion cuisine and broadened her repertoire by including European, African, and East and West Asian dishes. I wanted to learn how she made these delicious and delightful dishes, with their delicate balance of minced onions, garlic, tomatoes, herbs, and spices, that she served to us as children.

The oldest cookbook known to humankind was discovered in Baghdad and is over ten thousand years old. In its pages are recorded the recipes of our culture, recipes we still use to this day and are very often prepared in the same way. Although the word "ancient" is often misused to describe a nation that no longer exists, in the case of our knowledge, there is pride in knowing it is both ancient and modern. Through food I began to find myself deeply connected with my culture. Every visit to Lebanon was an opportunity to collect spices, oils, dried flowers, and other traditional ingredients needed to continue exploring Lebanese cuisine abroad. I wanted my kitchen to smell like my great-grandmother's kitchen.

I hope to regain and master all the knowledge of my grandmother and great-grandmother and all my ancestors, from our food to all the discredited knowledge that is passed down from women to girls through culture and tradition. Granted, some of this education we must unlearn, or rather heal, but much of the knowledge passed down through Indigenous culture and tradition is what makes women of the Global Majority the catalysts of change. We know how to care for and elevate our communities through food, ritual, and spiritual knowledge, making us the perfect agents for our collective liberation.

NOTES

8. The term migraine was adopted in 1970. The World Federation of Neurology's Migraine and Headache Research Group published a definition of migraine as "a familial disorder characterized by recurrent attacks of headache that vary widely in intensity, frequency, and duration."

CHAPTER IV

International Solidarity

The Water is Sacred

Cassette #4: "Khalas"

The song by Ziad Rahbani is playing on the radio of the car, an oriental jazz tune with absurd Lebanese slang lyrics. Khalas means "that's it, it's over."

Summer 2000 – Lebanon

We were in my boyfriend's car. I had successfully lied to my parents. I told them I was going to be spending the weekend with Hala. I looked at my boyfriend; he was smoking while eating a licorice candy, his signature combo.

I asked casually, attempting to mask my excitement, "Where are we going?"

He smirked.

"Where are we going?" I feigned indifference by staring out the window and admiring the flowers and pine trees that adorned the Lebanese mountains. I noticed the brilliant sunset, its bright pink and yellow hues filtering through the pines—colors typical of this region in Lebanon.

"You're going to a military-style training camp," he stated, breaking my reverie.

"What?!" Trying to control a growing panic in my chest, I demanded clarification.

Even though we'd been dating for a year, we had just recently become exclusive. He was older—in university while I was still in high school—and handsome, a total rebel, a wild card, an unpredictable and mysterious but utterly fascinating person. He was knowledgeable in Lebanese and regional history and had introduced me to so much knowledge through his passion for geopolitics and the larger political landscape, something the adults in my family would never go into detail about given the sectarian strife and horrors of the war they had all lived through.

The fact that he had chosen me as his Official Girlfriend was like a fairy tale come true to me. I'd concluded many years earlier that I was hard to love. That he wanted me, loved me, and that I had something to do with it was extremely satisfying. However, the bliss of teenage romance began to take a turn I wasn't expecting. Being taken against my will to a military-style training camp was not exactly what love meant to me.

"If you really love me, you'll do it," he said.

At the same moment, my Nokia phone alerted me of an incoming text message. My mother asked, "Everything OK?"

The panic I was trying to control was set loose; nonetheless, I lied, "Yes, Hala and I are together, talk to you later!"

I could no longer hide my frenzy and began to demand that we turn around and that I be taken home immediately.

My boyfriend smiled. He was in control and had no intention of freeing me. Not without a fight. That same summer on a weekend trip where I'd lied to my parents that I was with the same Hala (who was becoming less and less a friend), he'd taken me to the Palestinian border where we'd gotten into a serious car accident and almost died. I was so crazy in love with him that I forgave him then and for so many of the unspeakable things he'd done to me.

I had no idea where we were, only that we were driving up a mountain on an endless road. Constant twists and turns revealed a repetitive scene of pine trees, rocks, red earth, and gray stone homes, giving me vertigo and making me feel nauseated all at once. (Perhaps this was one of the roads my grandfather had opened many years ago.) As my boyfriend drove, I pleaded for my freedom to no avail. Crying and screaming the entire drive, I was completely exhausted and momentarily surrendered when we finally arrived at the campsite.

We parked in the middle of the forest where the red earth is bed for hundreds of thousands of centuries-old trees: stone pines, mahaleb cherry trees, Lebanon oaks, Turkey oaks, kermes oaks, Greek junipers, carob trees, Syrian pear trees, and of course the iconic cedars that have been famous in the region for thousands of years, from which the Canaanites made their boats to travel the known world. The biodiversity of our forests has survived thousands of years of colonial rule by empire after empire, as well as a fifteen-year-long war that compromised the national cedar population. In these forests lived wildcats, striped hyenas, jackals, Egyptian mongooses, least weasels, beech martens, European otters, Caucasian badgers, honey badgers, gray wolves, marbled polecats, caracals, red foxes, porcupines, and squirrels.

I had never slept in a forest. Camping was not a part of my family culture. I would argue that it would have been a rare occurrence for my family (and many like my own) to voluntarily venture into the wilderness to sleep unprotected in tents given all we'd had to live through between the wars and forced displacement as refugees. That the campsite had quite a few tents set up and several large water tanks for showers installed, as well as speakers mounted on a few trees around the site blasting old Fairuz songs, was both creepy and comforting.

Although I was unable to stop crying, I felt a sense of relief learning I would be sharing my tent with three girls my age: two sisters from Syria and one girl from Palestine by way of Jordan. Inside the tent, I was given a polyester blanket with tigers and flowers printed on it to sit on. It was a typical blanket style in our part of the world, and something I found deeply comforting in that moment. I felt the tigers were looking out for me.

The Palestinian girl began sharing her story to distract me and connect with me. Her family had been forced to leave her native home in Palestine by the Israeli Occupying Military Forces. Her native home was near a freshwater well where her neighbors often gathered to collect water and socialize. One day she was awakened before dawn to the terror and chaos of Israeli soldiers barging into her house. They harassed her and her family and then kidnapped her brother. She and her family were given only a few minutes to gather the possessions they could carry before they were forced to leave their home for good. The well was what she seemed to miss the most. "Water is sacred. It was our home."

My years in Montreal as a refugee made me completely unaware of the struggles my peers had been facing for decades while living under occupation—all the stories ended up tracing their origins back to the Israeli occupation and the US and UK backing it. My tentmates shared more of their stories, explaining that they were passionate about learning how to fight for our collective liberation. Even though I was feeling a deep sense of betrayal, I was also grateful I had the chance to meet these women. We immediately felt connected to each other and bonded over stories of war, hardship, and loss. I could feel their solidarity with me.

I listened to their stories of water with intense fascination. The Israeli Occupying Forces had a practice of tracking and taking control of the water sources. One of the Syrian girls shared that many times during the war the Israeli soldiers deliberately polluted the well water, a common tactic employed by invaders and colonial forces. In Lebanon the consequences of this tactic—as well as the repeated destruction of water treatment plants—is that, to this day, we have very little potable water. In addition to polluting wells, the previous French colonizers had a habit of driving Lebanese inhabitants out of the areas that were richest in freshwater resources.

"You'll learn so much during this five-day camp," one of the sisters exclaimed.

Five days! My phone will run out of power and my parents will definitely know I was lying to them when they call Hala to ask about me. And I know she won't protect me.

"Self-defense and political knowledge are the keys to our liberation," the other sister explained while handing me a tissue to dry my tears.

"But I was brought here against my will!" I replied through jagged sobs.

"It's for your own good."

"My own good? You're talking about our liberation, and you're okay with me being abducted and forcibly brought here by a guy? For my own good?"

The debate went nowhere. I insisted I had a right to my own sovereignty, and they insisted I should be grateful for the experience I was about to have. Fairuz's voice blasted through the forest, her endless lamentations, her compassionate soul reverberating through my tired body, as I wept and wept.

We were finally summoned to unite outside. We left the safety of the tent and my tiger blanket and joined the community gathered around the campfire, where we were instructed to sit directly on the red earth. (The earth in Lebanon has a reddish color because of the rich levels of iron and minerals in the soil.) We all sat cross-legged and were each given a pita bread—not the thick, doughy pancakes found in American groceries stores, but the thin, soft, two-layer kind found in Lebanese, Syrian, Palestinian, and Jordanian culture. Each of us held our pita open, waiting to receive a scoop of MaLing canned meat (a staple during the Lebanese war), along with a few chunks of tomato, a slice of lemon, and a pinch of salt. We were then served warm chai to wash it down.

I felt both loved and betrayed all at once, which is a typical feeling for a Lebanese person. The contradiction is real, and quite frankly, we Lebanese are able to understand the deepest forms of contradiction on a visceral level. That is where we often live, somewhere between fighting and loving. I ate quietly and sipped my tea, feeling this uncomfortable yet familiar inner contradiction while listening to my newfound peers debating political concepts tied to our shared history.

I learned I was at a training camp for a political party, based on the concept that the people of the Levant, from southern Türkiye down to Palestine, from the Mediterranean to Persia, comprise one larger ethnolinguistic group with shared culture and history that predate the Abrahamic religions and have survived the Arab and European conquests. The camp was about building a multifaith unity and solidarity in the region to rediscover and strengthen this shared culture in opposition to the larger geopolitical forces seeking to divide and control our region. And although they didn't use the word, it was inherently about our innate right to sovereignty as the Indigenous people of these lands.

The older Syrian sister spoke passionately about the party, saying it was the only group striving for the unity of our region. The party wanted us to be proud of our history as the people of the Fertile Crescent and the

Levant, to be proud that we were descendants of the oldest civilizations on earth, the civilizations that created the ancient Zoroastrian, Sumerian, and Canaanite religions, which are the direct antecedents of Judaism, Christianity, and Islam.

"We are all one people," she said, "and we must unite to drive out everyone who is trying to create war and chaos in our land. This includes Israel, which was founded by Europeans and Russians who came conquering with the British, who created chaos in Lebanon in 1948 with all the Palestinian refugees driven out by massacre and by force, and again in 1967, who invaded Lebanon in 1982 and at this time still occupies parts of the south of Lebanon with the help of the US who funds and supports their military and their illegal annexation of land from Palestine, Jordan, and Lebanon."

Later, the younger Syrian sister, who had a more nuanced view of the party, spoke of the importance of separating the Zionist-military-industrial project from Judaism and Jewish culture. She told me that even though it is a primary tactic of European and Russian Zionist terrorists to commit massacres and steal land in the name of all Jews, we must remain very clear that the fight is against Zionists and Zionism, not Jews and Judaism so that they cannot use false claims of antisemitism to discredit our anti-colonial stuggle. We oppose Zionist occupation, just as we opposed the French and British invasion and occupation of the Levant. That year I was studying philosophy and diving into the issues of identity, nationalism, and colonialism. I argued wholeheartedly that anti-colonialism could not be based on an idea of racial superiority, or any microdivision that serves the divide-and-conquer mandate of a larger ruling class. These ideas have remained core to my philosophies to this day. So many times we see those who are fighting oppression of some type turn their aggression on those who should be peers.

I considered running away. I began taking inventory of the cars parked near the side of the deserted unpaved road. I took a short walk alone after dinner to survey the perimeter and identify ways I could safely run away. When the time came to go to bed, my boyfriend appeared out of nowhere to say good-bye and wish me luck. He repeated that this was for my own good and would make me into a warrior. I was beyond furious; I was livid. I started yelling at him, punching his chest, and demanding that he take me back to Beirut with him. The men in charge came to his defense, silencing me and pulling me into another section of the camp to "talk some sense into me," as they put it. I was hysterically crying by then and begging for my freedom.

Everyone in charge demanded that I go back to my tent, brush my teeth, and go to sleep. I had to obey them, mainly because there was a looming threat that if I didn't, some sort of military training-inspired torture was available to straighten me out. With my head low and my eyes swollen from crying, I returned to my tent, washed my face with cold water to appease my eyes, brushed my teeth, and went to sleep. I was so exhausted that as soon as I closed my eyes, I was gone.

The next morning we were awakened at 5 a.m. by free-roaming roosters, who would eventually become dinner later in the week. I opened my eyes and looked around the tent.

As my vision adjusted to the dim predawn light, I locked eyes with one of the girls who was already awake.

Smiling and enthusiastic, she said, "Sabaho!"

"Sabah El Kheir," I responded, still in shock.

She looked at me with compassion and said, "Just give it some time here, you'll be grateful."

The sun hadn't even risen yet, but in our tent the morning sun was beaming from her eyes. In Arabic we call this *Nawarit*, which means "the light you bring." All my tentmates were so joyful. I couldn't understand their joy, but they all shared so much love for Lebanon, and for being here on its soil. In Arabic we hold a lot of importance for the soil, the sand, the earth of a given place. We worship the soil. Many Fairuz songs are about the soil of Palestine and the soil of Beirut. And speaking of Fairuz, the speakers began blasting her laments, which rose higher and higher into the dawn and through the slowly awakening forest. It was time to get up.

One of my tentmates grabbed my hand and said, "Habibti, strengthen yourself."

I nodded as I ducked out of the tent, ready to start the new day. We gathered in the middle of the forest by the fire. We were given a cup of warm water, a packet of Nescafé, and a small spoon to mix the powder into the water. There was also an option to have hot milk made with hot water and powdered milk. Nescafé and powdered milk were the survival staples used during and after the war. Though Turkish coffee is available and prepared multiple times per day, the remnants of European rule continue to include serving comfort food: Nescafé, La Vache qui rit, Nido powdered milk, and canned Spam—all nostalgic parts of the fabric of our homes during war. Even in the middle of nowhere, in a forest overlooking lush green mountains, we were at home sipping Nescafé, and we felt it.

Then we all received a large pita bread that we opened and prepared, ready to receive the offering of the day: a scoop of labneh. In Lebanese cuisine, labneh—a type of salty, thickened yogurt—is a staple, a delicacy, and a medicine all at once. It contains a high level of probiotics for gut health and for healing any stomachache. After the labneh was evenly spread across the rounded edges of the pita, the zaatar was sprinkled generously, followed by a river of olive oil, tomatoes, cucumbers, and olives. As I was rolling my pita, slowly and delicately, I couldn't help but feel a deep sadness within my throat. I wasn't sure how I was going to eat, and I certainly didn't want to attract any more attention at this point as I continued to plan my escape. I took a first bite, mostly empty bread with a pinch of labneh, and deliberately chewed, trying to make time go as slowly as possible so I could process what was happening to me. My brain was on overdrive; I had to figure out how to get out of there.

After breakfast we were separated into groups and taken on hikes in the forest. After two hours hiking, we began the survival workshop, which included commando crawl. We did this a few dozen times, enough for me to swallow some dirt. I was filthy by then, between the hike, the crawl, and all the times sitting on the ground. I was covered in dirt, but it felt oddly grounding. The training showed us how to camouflage ourselves, avoid bullets by hiding behind rocks, and find refuge in bushes. We also did push-ups, sit-ups, leg raises, and jumping jacks. We then hiked back to the site and sat near the fire again where we were offered water and chai. The same pita bread ceremony followed, but I couldn't eat this time.

Next, we were gathered under a tree for dialectic thinking and political education. I remember debating the entire time, the debate escalated, and I stood up to argue passionately against what seemed to be their core beliefs: (1) that we need to go back in time to move forward, which ignored the displacement of so many, (2) the validation of the persecution of Palestinians, and (3) the adoption of patriarchy and the limited role of women in the movement. Even though women were front and center as revolutionaries, their role remained limited in the political arena. I debated with the boys in the group, who found it quite entertaining to try to school me into obedience. I debated until the sun went down and it was time to sing Arabic songs tied to the movement, none of which I knew.

I spotted my boyfriend in the distance, jauntily walking down the hill from where his car had just been parked.

He'd returned to check on his captive. I wanted to punch his satisfied face. I stood up and ran toward him. He tried to hug and kiss me, but I immediately pushed him away.

"Take me home now or I'm going to make such a scandal you'll regret it!" My phone battery had already died. I desperately needed to contact someone, maybe his parents?

I reached for his back pocket, but he put his hand on my hand.

"I need to text my family."

"No, you can't."

I started wrestling with him. He pulled my arms behind my back and said, "If you really loved me, you'd do this with grace."

I burst into tears and said, "If you really loved me, you'd give me the freedom to choose!"

I rushed back to the group, feeling completely helpless and needing the support of my tentmates.

One of the Syrian sisters asked, "What's wrong?"

I was silently sobbing and couldn't talk.

"You did so well today!"

"Is he your boyfriend?"

I nodded, then uttered "tsuk" while raising my eyebrows, a sound and facial expression that signifies "no" in our culture.

Before we went to sleep, the girls and I washed ourselves with freezing water from big plastic gallon jugs. The outside temperature had dropped significantly, and though the water felt like ice, it was a balm on my face, especially around my eyes, which were red, raw, and puffy from all the crying. We then filled our water bottles from containers reserved for potable water. Lebanese people have suffered from water shortages ever since the war began. Clean drinking water is simply not available in Lebanese homes. It doesn't come out of the taps and is not provided by the government. Transporting gallons of water up and down our stairs is normal; we have always relied on bottled water. The luxury of easily accessible clean drinking water is something my generation has never known.

Once we'd returned to the tent, the girls began whispering about first kisses, secret love affairs, and sex. As they shared stories, my mind wandered. I could only think about how to safely get back to Beirut. *Maybe I could walk the path until I reached the road? Where were we anyway? Which part of Lebanon?* I truly had no idea. I excused myself and left the tent. I walked toward the location where the adults were staying—the chef and the leaders of the party and their wives. As I approached, I could see them sitting on white plastic chairs smoking cigarettes, *arguilé* (hooka), and drinking chai.

I walked with conviction as I spotted the laughing face of my boyfriend. He looked in my direction and began to walk toward me.

"You're calmer now?" he asked.

"No, I'm not calmer. I'm going to denounce you for having abducted me. I'm going to let them all know what you did, and that my parents did not consent to this. That you took me without my knowledge or my consent and that you forced me to be here!" I was determined. "I will not be sleeping here tonight. I'm returning to Beirut."

The leaders heard me and began to walk toward us. "Is it true that she's here without her parents' consent?" one of them asked.

I looked into his eyes with a fire burning around my entire being. I was going to leave that night; I would make it happen. Either my boyfriend would drive me back, or I would walk through the dark until I found the road. And if I got killed on my way home, at least I'd die a free woman. I was seventeen years old and had already felt very close to death at multiple times in my short life. This path, out there, did not scare me anymore. I insisted that if I called my father, if anyone would let me borrow their cell phone, I could prove to them I was brought there without his knowledge.

Somehow that seemed to work better than my previous narrative claiming I was brought to the camp against my own will. That didn't seem convincing enough, but my father's not knowing about this abduction somehow made them fear God for a second. I started asking frantically for a cell phone to make a call.

I approached the women, the wives. Sobbing again, I pleaded, "Please, can I make a phone call?" The women were clearly afraid to help me, unsure of what to do. Even after looking each one of them in the eyes, not one made a move to help me. I desperately wanted to leave that place.

I rushed back to my tent, leaving them perplexed. I started gathering my things. My roomies were surprised to see my determination but knew to respect it. They helped me gather my belongings.

"Are you sure you want to leave?" one of them asked.

I was more than sure.

"This is the training you need to survive, sister," another offered.

I looked at them, filled with anger and love and regret, and said, "I want to leave now!"

They nodded to show they'd heard me, but I knew they didn't approve. However, I didn't need collective approval at this time, I just needed to honor my spirit.

"Bye, take care," I said, hugging each of them tightly. They hugged back even tighter.

I flew back to where my boyfriend was standing. He was smoking a cigarette while eating a licorice candy, as always. (He called it *bambouné*, which is the word for candy in Arabic slang. It's actually *bombonné*, a play on the French word *bonbon*, and an intentional butchering of the pedantry of the French pronunciation. *Bambouné* was his exaggeration with a pronunciation borrowed from elders living deep in our mountains.)

When our eyes met, I made a motion that indicated, "Let's go."

He pulled my arm and tried to reason with me, saying it was disrespectful of me to want to leave like that, that I was making a scene. That I looked unhinged, crazy. As he pulled me closer, he tried to hold my head and kiss me. I know this may sound terrible, but I was melting in his arms. I was seventeen and completely in love with him. He was a revolutionary who had lived through and survived a war I had escaped, and here I was trying to run away.

Being so close to him, I could reach for his cell phone and in a split second had managed to pull it out of his pocket and speed dial his father. He tried to pull the phone out of my hands, but I was contorted in a way to keep the phone out of reach.

I heard, "Allô?"

I said, "I'm stranded in a military camp, your son is forcing me to stay here, it's Céline."

My boyfriend managed to pull the phone away from me and hang up. He was stunned. I took my bag and walked toward the leader's campsite. This time it was game over. I was leaving.

"You're taking me home now!" I screamed. This time letting myself reach new levels of madness. He already thought I was crazy, but I would show him what I was truly made of.

His cell phone started ringing; his father was calling him back. He answered, but I couldn't hear what his father was saying, only how my boyfriend responded.

"No, it's all good, there's nothing here, she's exaggerating."

I jumped on his arm and screamed into the phone, "No! I'm not exaggerating, I'm in a forest in the middle of nowhere in a military camp! Please tell your son to drive me back to Beirut, please!"

I kept repeating that I wanted to leave, over and over again. I was completely traumatized. I felt violated.

Finally, we got in my boyfriend's car. He was furious and gave me the silent treatment for the first hour, then began yelling insults at me. He accused me of humiliating myself and him with my childish behavior. I cried, thinking I'd lost his respect because I'd chosen my own freedom. But the truth was, and I knew it, that he never really respected me in the first place.

As we drove down the twists and turns of the mountain road, the Mediterranean Sea started to peek through the trees at dawn. When we finally got to the coastline, the sea began to sparkle as the sun rose above the horizon and I began to weep, not for the loss of my relationship, but with relief. I was free.

Following the Water

Reverence for fresh water is a cultural value shared across all the religions of my land. In Lebanon every single fresh spring and river is connected to a divinity. In Christian areas, *Ein* (freshwater springs) are blessed with a sculpture of a saint to watch over them. In Islam, water sources are also sacred and often present in front of or near mosques. The relationship between deities and water predates the rise of the Abrahamic religions—so many of the early religions of the area center around rivers and fresh water—and is present in *hammams* and bath culture.

Water is deeply understood as the source of all life. The stories shared with me in the tent about how occupying colonial forces targeted and poisoned or claimed water sources showed me the difference between life-loving, Indigenous cultures and the occupying colonial forces. Just as Ottoman conquerors threw dead animals into wells to poison them, to this day the Israeli army fills in Palestinian wells with concrete.

Water was the theme of an important initiative for my organization, Slow Factory. In 2022, we were invited to Hawai'i to join forces with the O'ahu Water Protectors, a group of Kānaka Maoli (Indigenous Hawai'ian) resistance organizing to protect the water on O'ahu. The only freshwater aquifer on the island was being polluted by the US military in Kapūkakī (Red Hill). Fuel tanks holding hundreds of millions of gallons of jet fuel that were installed during WWII had been left in disrepair for decades, and recently leaked tens of thousands of gallons of fuel into the island's main aquifer. The colonial playbook is similar everywhere in the world where colonizing forces are deployed to seize control. Sacred sites, often connected to freshwater sources, are frequently targeted and occupied by the colonial military; we have seen this pattern from O'ahu all the way to Palestine. Oftentimes these water sources are left polluted or dried up. In essence, they are destroyed. This was the situation in O'ahu and the reason we were invited to participate.

During our time there, we gathered information, exchanged tactics of resistance and solidarity, and worked to publicize the crisis globally, to shine a light and international pressure on the injustices occurring at the hands of the US military. While we were still on site working, we learned that key data and information as to the extent of the spill was gathered but then withheld from publication by the University of Hawai'i—pressure from Slow Factory and the Water Protectors lead directly to this key data being released. Although the Navy continued to deny the severity and evade accountability for the spill, continued pressure has led the Navy to finally accept and put forward a plan to repair and completely defuel the facility.

Although we were invited to Hawai'i by a group of Indigenous people to support their struggle, the work in O'ahu was particularly delicate. Coming from "the continent," we were keenly aware that tourism on the Islands is discouraged by Indigenous communities who have been fighting for their rights since the Islands were colonized by the US. None of our team had ever been to Hawai'i previously, partly for this very reason.

This important work was part of our Deep Ecology program at Slow Factory, which entails acknowledging the connections between Indigenous peoples and cultures across the world with the intention of creating a body of work that documents and inspires collective action, resilience, and creativity. The Deep Ecology program in O'ahu in relation with the O'ahu Water Protectors began as an exploration of water and resistance, and very quickly became more concrete when I shared my desire to create an initiative with Dr. Uahikea Maile, Kānaka Maoli scholar, activist, and practitioner from Maunawili, Oʻahu. He was at the time assistant professor of Indigenous Politics in the Department of Political Science at the University of Toronto, St. George, and has given an Open Edu class with Slow Factory called "Land and Indigenous Politics." When we were in Oʻahu, he taught a class called "Oʻahu Water Crisis: Shut Down Red Hill!"

When we arrived in Oʻahu, a member of the Slow Factory team, Paloma, our community lead, booked a Reiki (energetic) session with someone she knew and trusted. We drove to meet everyone on the beach, where beneath a rain-drenched sunset we received a Reiki healing. During the session we were invited to connect with our ancestors, ask for guidance, and then share what came forward for each of us in the session. The word *healing* came up for me. *Interconnectedness* came up for Nicole, our project lead, *strength* for Josh, our researcher and writer, and *solidarity* for Colin, my partner in both life and work. We definitely needed these reminders; we were about to embark on a week of intense experiences.

Slow Factory's core team consisted of a mixed group of Arab women including myself, an Afro-Indigenous woman, and two men, both of white European backgrounds one of which is Jewish. Upon arrival at the farm, we were invited to witness a traditional Hawaiʻian welcoming ceremony. To see Indigenous peoples honor their Indigenous knowledge and to hear their songs sung in their native language is sacred. It was a great privilege to be invited to witness it. To preserve and respect the sacredness of the knowledge shared, I won't go into the details of this important experience, but I will say that it highlighted for me how detribalized folk like Lebanese, Syrians, and Palestinians have lost some of their native songs as their native languages have been replaced by Arabic. In Lebanon, for example, Aramaic is still spoken in some ancient churches, but through the centuries, Arabic, then French, and now increasingly English have replaced native languages.

It is important to understand some of the fundamental context of the history of Hawai'i. The 1893 coup d'etat and 1898 annexation of the Kingdom of Hawai'i by US forces have had a devastating effect on the Indigenous population of Hawai'i. There are over 14 military bases in Hawai'i, with most of them located in O'ahu. Military activities, such as the storage, leakage and dumping of jet fuel and chemicals like PFAS, have resulted in the contamination of water sources on the islands. Incidents of chemical contamination have led to health issues for residents, including birth defects and mental health concerns. Because of invasive plantations and tourism, the water has been progressively rerouted away from natural ecosystems and Indigenous people.

We visited the Mākua Valley, a gorgeous land by the ocean that has been occupied by the US Military since the 1920s and used to test out many munitions that were later used in Palestine, Lebanon, Syria and around the world. There are almost a thousand US military bases in the world used to enable US control of various regions around the globe via proxy wars and other corporate interests.

Front line activism forces various groups of people from different backgrounds to come together in solidarity for a given urgent cause. Our work for climate justice is often in relationship with water, air, soil or access to food and energy. In most cases we invite and create spaces where people from different ethnicities and socioeconomic backgrounds are invited to collaborate together. In an ideal world, everyone would come together harmoniously like the culture I experienced with my tentmates.

We have not ever before, in our shared human history, been called or required to share space with one another while mobilizing for an existential threat that affects us all. This is new territory. Our generation must document and create a body of work with insights on nurturing, healing, and creating solidarity as an experimental blueprint on how to create shared space for colonized peoples and their emancipation. To convene with the intention of fostering solidarity, we must embrace compassion, healing, and the expansion of our imaginations in order to create liberation. We just don't have all the tools yet, and the framework used is often borrowed from the handbook of colonial praxis and theory, reinforcing division and hierarchies based on ideas of purity.

Solidarity sits between compassion and loyalty—loyalty grounded in shared values that are ultimately designed for the well-being of the collective. Solidarity is not taught to us in schools; in fact the school system fosters individualism and a sense of competitiveness. In the workforce, solidarity can disrupt one's ability to rise up the corporate ladder. Individual efforts are rewarded while collective action, such as participating in unions, is condemned. In a capitalist society, loyalty is to the dollar. In spaces dedicated to collective causes, from climate to social justice, solidarity most often exists in a tribal state. "Which social group do you belong to?" Solidarity has been, for hundreds of years of survival under colonial rule, intimately tied to collective survival.

Being able to imagine other ways of being, in this context, is a privilege, given that colonialism is not a thing of the past; it is an economic and political reality for most people in the world. Having the ability to question and imagine alternative ways of being is a responsibility we take seriously at Slow Factory. We work hard to build safe spaces where we provide the necessary bandwidth to question, explore different avenues of thought, and gain a level of perspective and clarity.

Our lived experiences are paved with wisdom and knowledge that can never be taught in schools. This kind of knowledge is often discredited, mocked, and diminished. This unacknowledged education offers the very knowledge that is needed for understanding and imagining new systems for generating original ways of thinking and reviving the multiplicity of languages and the variations in thought and ideas needed for us to thrive in this world. As we imagine and mobilize to create our collective liberation, we must learn to do this in the spirit of solidarity.

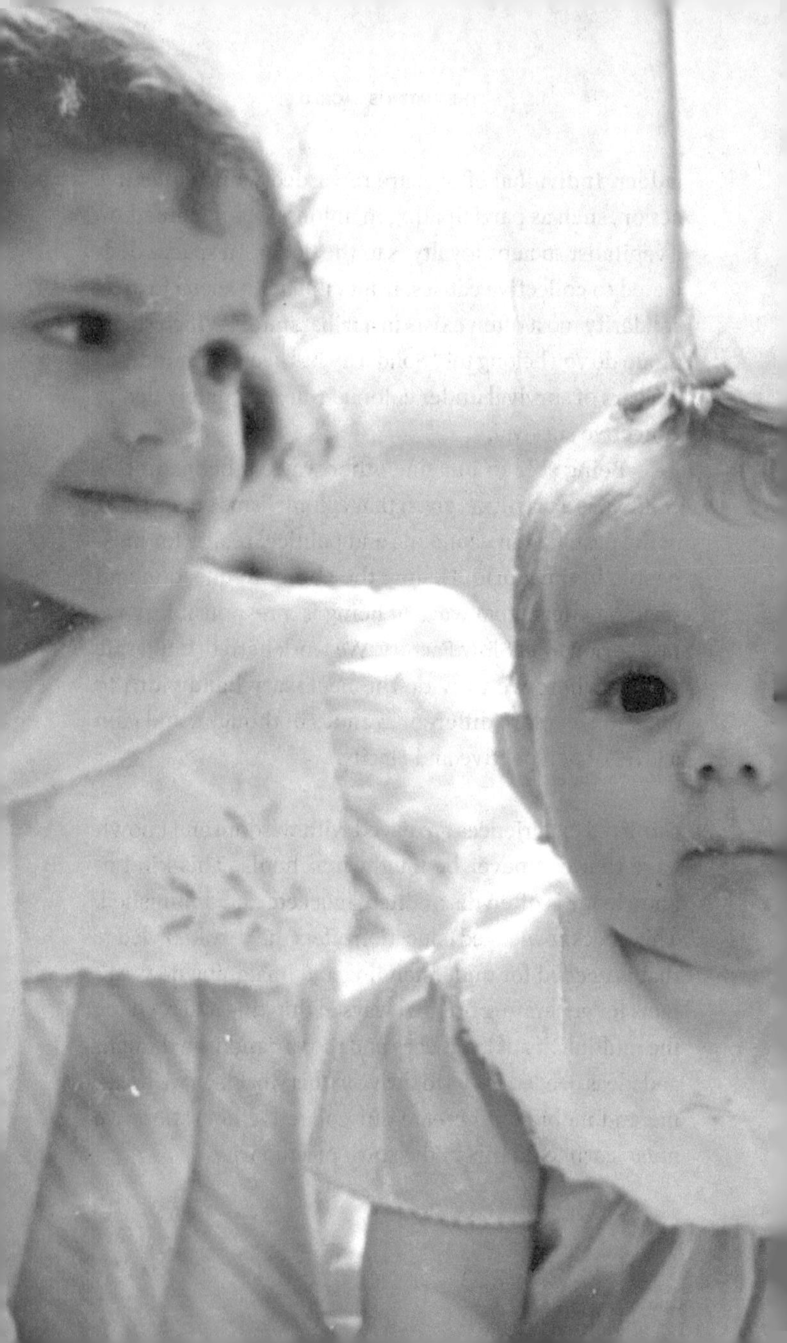

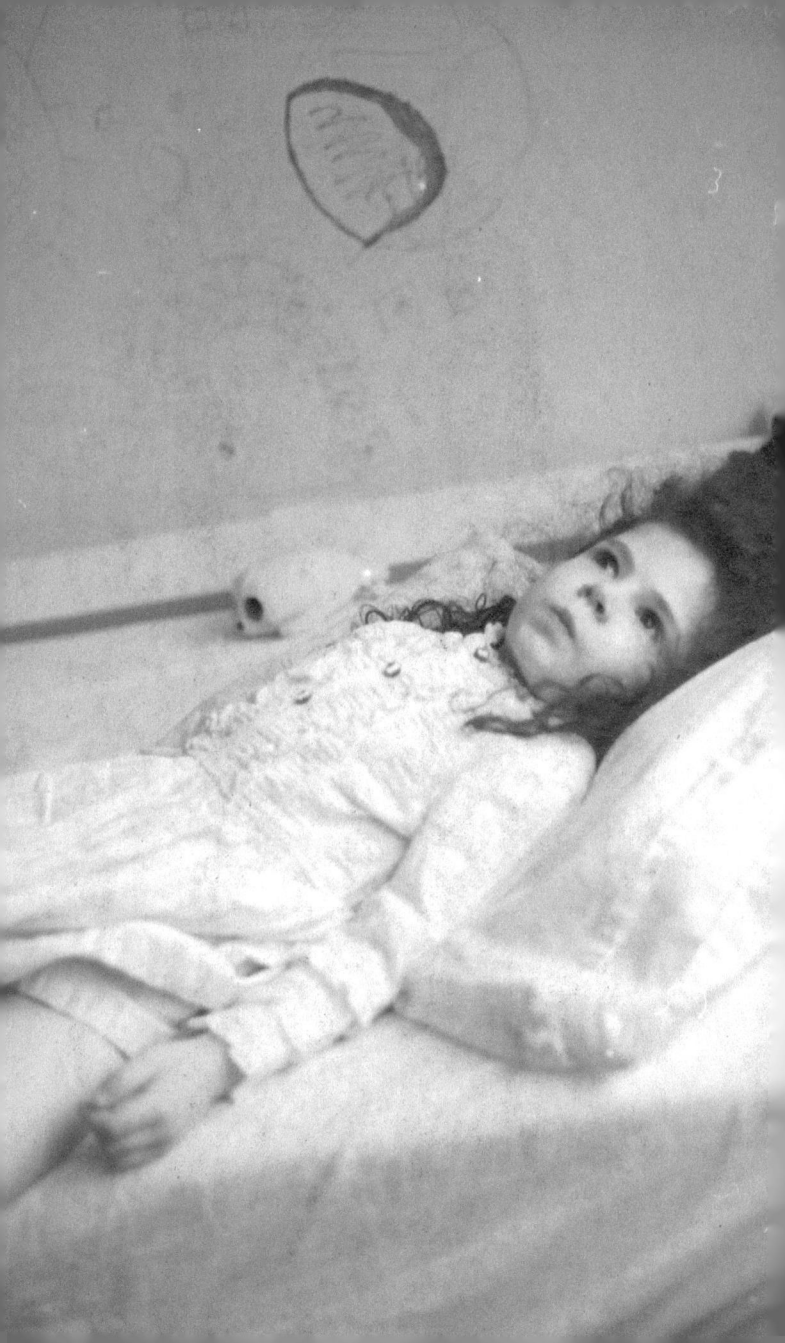

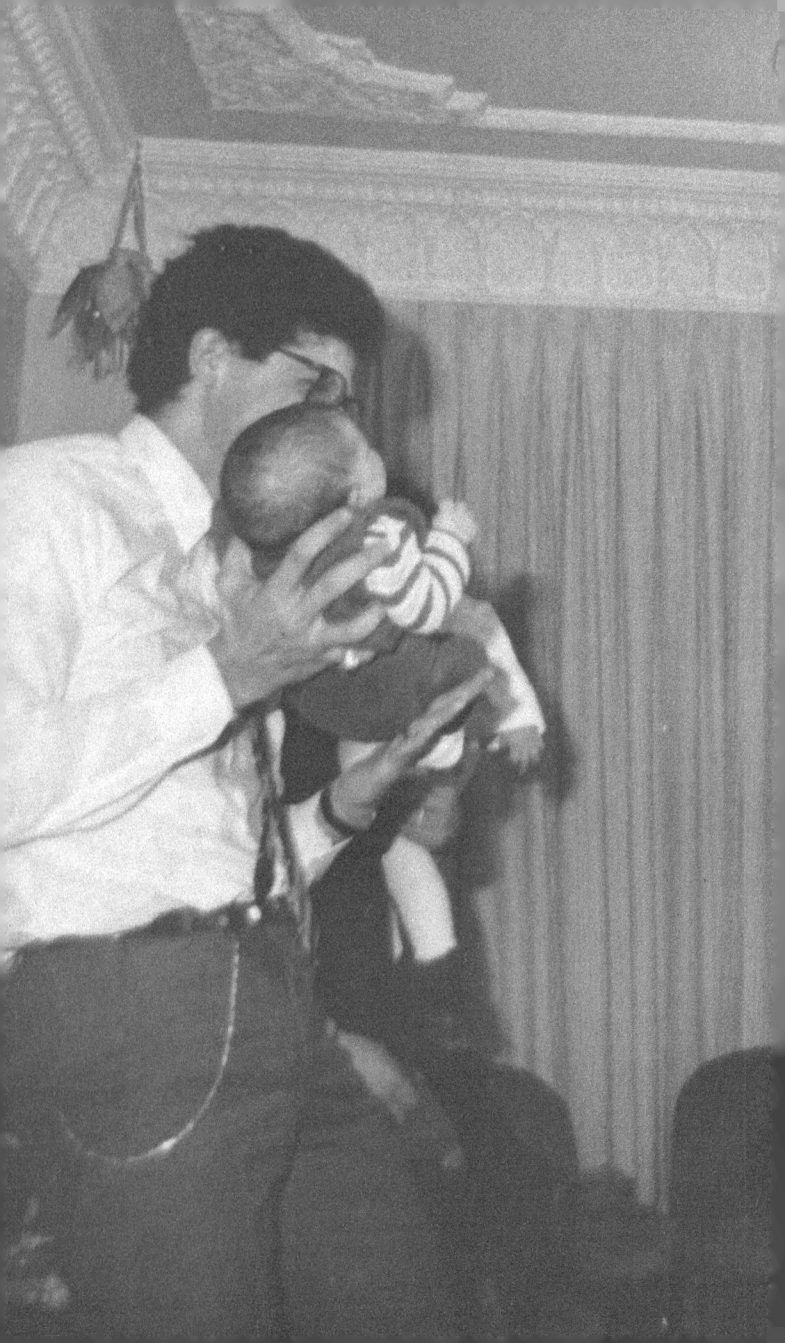

CHAPTER V

Global South, Baby

Cassette #5: "Habibi enta w ru7i enta"

*Played on the piano by my chain-smoking
Iraqi music teacher in Montreal, followed by
his voice narrating over it, singing the notes.*

Slap! The sound of her hand hitting my cheek reverberated through the square courtyard of the school. The courtyard was delineated by six marble pillars and surrounded by jasmine trees and gardenia plants. A crowd of students had gathered around us as the nuns walked slowly toward us, one of them holding a big bell and the other a clipboard with a whistle around her neck. The clapper hit the side of the copper mouth of the bell, creating a haunting rhythm as the sisters marched closer and closer.

It was 1998, a couple of years after my family and I had returned to Lebanon. I was almost sixteen and enrolled in a Catholic school run by nuns. It had the distinction of being somewhat more progressive than the first school I'd been enrolled in. Still fairly new and a total outsider, I felt the unbridgeable gap between myself and those who had been here their whole lives. My discomfort was apparent in the little mistakes I made in Arabic and the fact that I missed certain references and shared no collective memories. At the worst of times like this, my complete lack of understanding as to what it was like to grow up here solidified my outsider status.

My hand flashed to my cheek and remained there the entire time I was being confronted by Mariah. "How dare you come to us on your high horse, telling us to 'love thy neighbor' when we all, including you, have lost loved ones and continue to suffer from 'thy neighbor' you speak of!"

It was a rare moment when I didn't defend myself. I understood that what I'd said, though coming from an innocent place, was naive enough to be offensive to these teens, most of whom had not known a life without war until recently.

"'I love Muslim people, Jewish people, Christian people, and all people!'" She mocked my words. A tense laugh leaked from the crowd.

"You managed to escape during the war at some point, you didn't sleep in the shelters to the sound of your neighbors dying under bombs and grenades. At some point you were safe. You didn't see your brother's friend's hands exploding a split second after he touched an undetonated explosive in his garden. You didn't starve for days on end in the cigarette smoked-up shelters watching your parents rot in fear."

By then she was screaming. The nun's bell rang in my ear. Tears ran down my cheeks, despite all the hard labor my eye muscles were doing to hold them in, to save me even more humiliation. I closed my eyes, reeling as I processed the words. I felt suddenly like a traitor. *How dare I survive this war! How dare I forget where I came from?* Nine years of my life were spent in the Global North, being slapped by different hands for different reasons. I didn't belong here or there. Later in life, when I learned the words "survivor's guilt," the memory of the feeling of this day came flooding back to me.

The nun with the whistle around her neck, resting on her breasts next to her cross, lifted it to her lips and blew it with fervor, warning us to gather in one straight line to make our way back to our classrooms.

I opened my eyes and met Mariah's, staring intensely into mine. She may have just slapped me, schooled me in front of everyone, but she was still here looking at me, the anger and resentment in her eyes turning to compassion. She too had tears in her eyes, but her muscles were stronger than mine, hardened. Not a single drop ran down her cheeks. It was as if she were able to control water. Goddesslike, Ishtar living within her. She reached for my hand, held it tight as she walked me inside, back to our classroom. I was confused—*Didn't you just humiliate me? Why are you holding my hand?*—but I didn't dare speak. Her compassion served as a portal for my learning. Back in class I noticed that not a single person made fun of me. Instead, I received gentle gazes here and there, a few people winked at me, or nodded.

Being able to love through pain is what I was experiencing in Beirut. There needed to be an outlet for all the horror these children had endured. But their true hearts were constantly bleeding with love. I had already experienced other noteworthy slaps, and some less noteworthy. Physical slaps imprinted on my cheeks tied to transformative learning experiences. Learning experiences I would have loved to have gained without the slap.

I'd earned a slap previously from the hand of a nun. In 1996 when my family returned to Lebanon, I went straight into a Catholic school with a conservative French pedagogical system rooted in white supremacy and patriarchy. That's what I would say now; at the time I didn't have those words, only a feeling of repulsion for so many of the attitudes and teachings. For instance, we were taught to "be like Mary, Mother of Jesus: observe and be mute and pure, like her." What they omitted, and I learned only many years later, was that Mary had written a book of teachings after the murder of her son, which was rejected by the Romans who compiled the Bible. As a result, her book never made it into the final manuscript hundreds of years later when the Bible was assembled.

The colonial patriarchal system designated women like Mary to be servants. They rendered her mute, insisting on her virginity and purity, which forced generations of women after her into obedience and invisibility. At the other end of the spectrum, we find Mary Magdalene, branded as the whore—a myth created and propagated to demonize and control the Divine Feminine. The "other" Mary was shunned and degraded. I found both versions of Mary to be equally uncomfortable.

The nun who slapped me was inspired to violence by my simple insistence that "Mariam Magdalene wasn't a prostitute." What did I know of theology? Not much. But I knew she wasn't worthy of the contempt she was being painted with; I knew she wasn't a sinner. Even at that age I understood that sex work was work, and worthy of empathy not condemnation. Later I learned that vilifying sex and sex work as a sin is one of the fundamental violences of patriarchy. In fact, as my research later confirmed, Mary Magdalene was exalted and held a special place, most likely as Jesus's wife. Instinctively I knew she was a hero, an early Christian symbol of female empowerment before the culture was appropriated and transformed for the benefit of Imperial Rome.

This Catholic school was a remnant of the French colonial mandate, and we were force-fed self-hatred and colonial paradigms from 7 a.m. until 2 p.m. when we were finally allowed to get on the buses, still functioning after decades of use, to be driven home where infinite amounts of homework awaited us. Every morning we stood in front of the dying Christ reciting the "Our Father" and the "Hail Mary" in both Arabic and French. At first, I knew not a single word. I didn't even know how to properly make the sign of the cross. I would try mimicking the others, but I used my left hand, a gesture that garnered yet another slap. A quiet and generous indication of which hand to use would have sufficed. I'm a fast learner.

Contrast all this with the summer before I experienced all these different slaps. Living in Montreal, where my family had found refuge from the war in Lebanon nine years earlier, the slaps and hits and pushes I had experienced did not come with fundamentalist learnings. The only thing I learned from these Québécois slaps was that white people are racist. And that was not a lesson I needed a slap to learn. Even with a recurring and underlying atmosphere of racism and xenophobia, though, I was not prepared for the day when, at thirteen, the big news of the ceasefire in Lebanon came, and the next day, when my parents suddenly announced to my siblings and me that the war in Lebanon had officially ended and that we were returning to live there before the end of summer. It was as if a sandcastle somewhere in my being had collapsed. After this declaration of our imminent return to Lebanon, I felt as though I had briefly lost my hearing. My mind kept seeing scenarios of the times I was beaten up at recess and told to go back to where I came from.

I ran to my neighbor Jannette's house. She was one of the very first friends I'd made in Montreal. I ran there to let her know the news that I was leaving Montreal to go to Lebanon. I was terrified to go there, and she was terrified for me. She looked at me with immense pity. She never really thought much of me or my family; to her we came from a lesser world, a world where, as her mother put it, "people were unruly and didn't know how to live with one another." We were barbaric to them, and they would regularly remind me of my people's primitive nature.

I met Jannette in 1987, during the first year we lived in Montreal as refugees. I was running after the bus, late as usual, curls bouncing. When I reached the bus, she made it clear that I should go back to where I'd come from. The kids all erupted in laughter. Jannette created lots of games, one of them consisted of reaching into my big curly mane and plucking out one hair to carefully study in the sun. She was, in her racist and righteous way, entitled to study me as she pleased.

Examining the strand of hair, she'd exclaim, "How thick and curly!" She'd pull it taut between her fingers trying to break it and when she couldn't, she'd shriek, "How strong!"

The look of disgust on her face made it clear to me that my hair totally grossed her out. Not only that but the color of my hair resulted in a diagnosis of my humanity. She lamented with disdain at the depth of the blackness of my locks, how completely deprived of any brown hues it was. "How sad," she concluded, as if the color black meant death somehow. It was the blackest she had ever seen with her naked eye and because of that she would later determine I was part animal. How unfortunate!

My fate was in her hands, literally. And then to be surrounded by the laughter her game would incite was terrifying. Every day she played this game. The conclusions were always the same: I would be compared to all sorts of animals: sheep, boar, bears, it didn't matter. In retrospect, the repetition of this childish game felt far more violent to me than a slap ever did. I complained to my mother and aunt every now and then after school. I had many complaints. One of them was about how racist my teachers were. But the hair plucking and diagnosis that I was not human tortured me more fundamentally. I needed my mother to know.

My mother was constantly multitasking, either in the kitchen where she made every meal from scratch even if she'd worked on her feet all day, or with my siblings. She couldn't really hear me talking. I desperately needed her to acknowledge how violated I felt. When I made enough of a scene, she stopped cooking to look at me and say, "Tell this Jannette not to touch your hair ever again! Tell her that she isn't allowed to touch your hair! And if she touches your hair one more time, you, Céline, will be grounded. If you let her touch your hair, you'll be grounded for allowing her to do it." She would then pause theatrically and open her eyes so wide it looked as though her skull had suddenly swallowed her eyelids.

I was mortified by her response. I had to learn how to set my own boundaries or be severely grounded. This would, strangely, be the start of my friendship with Jannette, and through the years, I managed to set some boundaries and create somewhat of a safe space. After every playdate, I made an inventory of our differences. For instance, her family let her do anything she wanted. She was even able to get away with telling her parents to shut up. When I first witnessed this, I was stunned. Her world seemed free and beautiful, her golden hair unkempt yet flowing in the wind, her bare feet strutting on the pavement on our way to the corner store. She was like a little fairy. My siblings and I were definitely not allowed to walk on pavement with bare feet or tell our parents to shut up, or we would be subjected to Lebanese-level torture and punishment. My parents' signature punishment, besides beating our legs with wooden spoons, was forcing us to kneel on the pavement in front of the house with our hands held above our heads for hours until our limbs went numb.

Jannette feared both my mother and my auntie Nona who lived with us. Both would make sure we obeyed them. Their method was looking at us for an uncomfortably long time with their eyes wide open, without blinking. The expression was utterly terrifying, like someone looking through your soul. I have honored this legacy with my own children, and when I practice "the stare," I know they know that I know and that there will be no other way but my way. And they fear me just a little bit. It works without having to resort to any elaborate kind of punishment.

Jannette started weeping when I told her I was moving back to Lebanon, sucking all the tears away from me. I had to console *her* when all I wanted was someone to hold me while I cried. I was the one leaving a safe country to go live in one that appeared to be "hell on earth" as I was told by everyone I knew in Canada. I was scared of Lebanon. The reaction I got from her parents when they asked us why Jannette was crying was an expression of sheer horror. They were appalled, even saying they were sorry for me, adding, "It's too bad your people don't know how to live in peace."

During the time we lived in Canada, we'd only left once to go to Lebanon in 1992 as the war was officially winding down. I was ten, my sister was seven, and my brother three. We flew to Syria and were driven by the Syrian army across the border between Damascus and the Bekaa Valley. During the arduous ride to Beirut, we very quietly began singing lullabies to ourselves. The military man driving the vehicle turned his body toward us with a disturbing stare that demanded we shut up. Out the windows we saw endless rocky mountains under a starry sky, the headlights breaking the obscurity of the road we were taking. My sister fell asleep on me, my brother was sleeping on my mother, who was sitting in the back with us. We were all leaning gently on each other.

We finally made it to Beirut to visit my grandparents, who didn't know we were coming. When they made their way to the bottom of their building at two in the morning, they were stunned and then hysterical. I had never seen or experienced such a demonstration of joy and celebration. It was the middle of the night, yet it didn't matter. In fact, the entire neighborhood rose to welcome us warmly. Our grandparents kissed us everywhere, undoubtedly believing they would never see us again. We'd shown up unannounced in the middle of a war in the middle of the night. That's how my parents did things. It was always an elegant chaos.

Our grandparents even kissed us on our butt cheeks; I was astounded. In Arabic slang, people tease their children by celebrating their butts and farts and singing popular songs with lyrics proclaiming that diamonds are pooped out of their butts. It was that level of playful worship, the ultimate devotion of love. We were enveloped in the kind of love we had never experienced before. The kind of love that was unconditional, loud, unpredictable, mad, ridiculous.

It was August and Lebanon was an inferno of heat. The air was suffocating and there was no air-conditioning because there was no electricity most of the time. During the war, there were no air-conditioning units in homes anyway. We would drink water, eat watermelons, and sit on the balcony hoping for a breeze. Every so often, when we were graced with an errant breeze, my grandmother would bow to the ancestors and thank God. The sounds of the street vendors, the endless honking, the proximity of all the people everywhere was as suffocating as the hot air. It felt as if we were all being forced back into the womb of a giant mother. Comforting yet completely unsettling.

We were visiting at that time because Lebanon had called for a general ceasefire to take place during the first elections in twenty years. And, it just so happened, my auntie on my mother's side was getting married. She was twenty but had met her husband at fourteen by calling random numbers on the rotary telephone. Imagine: A prank call led to a relationship, and speaking daily during the war led to a marriage proposal. My uncle on my father's side was also getting married that summer to a woman he barely knew. Neither wedding ended up happening for different reasons. Nevertheless, we spent a month in Lebanon in the middle of a war on holiday—the only vacation I had ever known.

I tasted stretchy Lebanese ice cream, was given three brightly dyed baby chicks to raise (all of whom died on the balcony where we left them), and drove for hours with my family to visit sites of Lebanese saints in small grottos, roadside *mazars*,[9] monasteries, and cathedrals, and then luxuriated over four-hour meals in restaurants somewhere deep in the mountains. At the end of our holiday, I contracted meningitis and ended up staying for a few days in the hospital where my uncle worked. When I was well enough, we flew back to Montreal.

That day when it was announced we were to leave Montreal, my mother unceremoniously handed me a stack of empty boxes to pack for our permanent move back to Beirut. I collapsed on the floor and cried, consumed with a dreadful sense of loss. I packed my books first, then my collection of cherished cassettes, and finally the stack of CDs that had changed my life. I also packed a few of my favorite random objects: a cereal box prize with a picture of my sister's face on it (I still own this treasure), precious rocks such as pyrites and amethysts, and comic books. I lay on my bed and felt the entire Earth spinning me in circles.

The day we were to leave, Jannette came over, braided my hair, and gave me an envelope with letters to read on the plane. I had prepared letters too. We sat outside my home on the steps. This time in silence.

The first days in Lebanon felt like a nightmare to me. We were living with my grandparents in a small apartment in the Jdeideh neighborhood of Beirut. It's a nondescript area to the east outside the city center, and not particularly affluent. We kids were crammed together in the living room and my parents slept in my mother's childhood room. I felt their decision to move "home" was one neither of them had properly thought through. The same things we had experienced with the thrill of novelty during our short vacation a few years earlier felt empty and tasteless now. The stretchy ice cream in the rectangular cones, the pastel-colored chicks sold on the street that die the next day, the endless lunches and visits to the saints, were both upsetting and meaningless to me now. Inside I felt a kind of shame. I was now living in the "Third World."

I had completely internalized the idea of the Third World. At the time, there were no terms to respectfully describe anything that wasn't white, or that had been deliberately exploited and prevented from developing by European colonialism. Why would my parents uproot us again, this time from a safe country to one that was broken, where running water and electricity weren't even accessible? We gave up our home in Montreal to pile up like refugees in relatives' homes—something we had done for so many Lebanese families fleeing to Canada for a better life, and here we were doing it for what I could only see as a worse fate. It made no sense.

Everything had been going well for us in Montreal. My father had sold the gas station he began at when we first arrived and bought a small restaurant in a mall. He and my mother were creating new menus and making more money. We were doing well and had been able to move into a much nicer new home just a few years before our return to Beirut. Every weekend, my parents threw wild dance parties featuring Arab musicians. They would get all dressed up and dance and party with their friends until the sun rose. I was growing into my teens with hope and excitement, ready for high school and the new adventures there. Everything was amazing. I couldn't comprehend their decision to leave.

It was a massive culture shock for me to move to a postwar country I had little memory of and didn't identify with. The voice in my head, the one I had internalized from the Global North, was relentless. It criticized everything and was constantly nagging. We didn't have water for showering, or electricity to watch TV, or any friends to play with, or a safe place to even walk around. Everything was a threat in the beginning, and although Arabic was my first language, I wasn't even fluent anymore. I was immediately labeled as a foreigner. It was hard to blend in, particularly because I favored baggy jeans, crop tops, black nail polish, and a mopey expression. None of these were acceptable for a girl, and I was scolded by everyone, even people I didn't know. It was hell. I was reading Jean-Paul Sartre and truly feeling every vitriolic word. I was quick to judge and confront my parents, grandparents, cousins, and friends about "civility," progress, and societal evolution. Lebanon was clearly lowly in comparison to where I had become accustomed to calling home. My self-righteous speeches didn't last long before I either received a slap, or got yelled at, or both.

There was nothing to do but sit in a plastic balcony chair and look out at the neighborhood—at everyone passing by, at what they were doing and who they were with. I looked and considered whether they were cute, and if they were, where they lived. I was a teenager longing for connection. Someone, anyone I could connect with and talk to would have been a dream come true. Instead, I was sitting in the warm dusty air on a white plastic chair, watching the world pass by as if I were watching television.

One day early on I spotted a store not too far away that seemed to be open and looked like it had music, cassette tapes. I could easily walk there by foot. It wouldn't be too dangerous and I could be looked after from the balcony. This was my only hope! The cassette shop had mostly Arabic music and Western oldies from the sixties and seventies: The Beatles, Alice Coltrane, Elvis, Nina Simone. Some classics that I loved but that was pretty much it. I was devastated. I needed them to have something more current.

I asked, "Do you have Snoop Dogg, Dr. Dre, Madonna? Dance music?"

The shop keeper looked at me like I was from another planet. *What are you talking about?* was written all over his face. But he uttered no words, he just gave me that look.

I began to understand that after fifteen years of war, the entire country was stuck culturally and technologically in a time capsule that extended roughly from 1967 to 1979. The '90s had skipped Lebanon altogether.

As soon as I became aware of the music shop down the street, I was there every day. It became a daily ritual: I left the apartment in the late morning, bought a mulberry-flavored popsicle from the corner convenience store, and then headed to the music shop to see if anything new had arrived. I perused the badly printed covers of each of the new bootleg cassette tapes, sometimes bought one, and walked back home. On my way home I passed chickens risking their lives by crossing busy streets as they wended their way through the neighborhood, motorcyclists performing stunts on one wheel, and street vendors selling *kaak*,[10] vegetables, and cleaning products. I peered into the local hair salon where the hairdresser was busy turning every one of his customers into Arab versions of Marilyn Monroe. I also passed the occasional child walking to the store to buy cigarettes for their parents.

As I approached our building, I'd always stop to watch my grandfather Labib in the garage doing one thing or another, often welding metal for his sculptures.

I'd greet him with "Jeddo!"[11]

"Habibi!"[12] he'd shout. Then with a dance and a song in his voice, "Ahlan!"[13]

He'd invite me to walk through the garage back toward the entrance of our building where dark green marble covered the entire floor and ceiling. Although it was extremely hot outside, the marble kept the lobby of the apartment building cool. There was also a chilly breeze always coming from the stairs in the basement.

Pointing to the basement stairs one day, I asked, "Jeddo, where do the stairs go?"

"They lead to the shelters, you don't remember?"

I shook my head upward with a click of my tongue to indicate no.

With a wave of his hand he invited me to follow him. We went down the light gray polished marble stairs, which eventually gave way to unfinished stairs made of rough concrete that eventually descended into pitch darkness. The temperature dropped noticeably and I smelled dampness and dust. My grandfather produced a flashlight from somewhere and turned it on.

We were in a large unfinished concrete room that must have been the size of the entire building, a rough bunker or shelter. The room was scattered with low stools and wooden tables, and a few cigarette butts. The cold damp air felt thin as if there were not quite enough oxygen. We walked around in silence for a bit before he began to share stories. This neighbor's family and that neighbor's family and this other family in another neighborhood, all would gather here during specific raids on the neighborhood. I had come down here too when I was little—the life of the party apparently, performing dances and singing old Arabic songs, keeping everyone entertained and hopeful.

He and others in my family along with various neighbors must have spent many days and nights in this basement shelter while I was in Canada laughing and playing, chasing boys, or complaining about the endless hours I had to spend waiting around for my parents' store to close. Those places seemed so far away. My feelings of resentment made me feel like a spoiled child. I had no memory of this place, but the feeling I had as we walked around, as I heard my grandfather's stories, stayed with me—and came rushing back when I received that slap from Mariah a few years later.

"What did we eat down here?" I asked.

"Pita and Picon." Picon was a French processed cheese sold in small individually wrapped triangular wedges arranged in a circle nestled in a round box. During and after the war, Picon was a staple along with MaLing (canned ham) and za'atar with olive oil.

On our way back up the stairs, we emerged from complete darkness into bright white light that streamed through cinder blocks perforated with Arabic calligraphic shapes. We had a view first of the garden then into the neighbors' balconies and kitchens. We heard a man yelling at his wife, and a mother yelling at her son, a chicken or two fighting, and smelled the sweet aroma of food slowly cooking on someone's stove. The air warmed up and I began to breathe more easily in the oxygen-rich environment.

The elevator took us to our apartment, and my grandmother welcomed us with an exhilarating "Ya Ahla w Sahla!"[14] as if we hadn't seen each other in a very long time. She invited us to have coffee on the balcony.

The balcony was the place to be; my mother, aunts, and siblings were already gathered there. Everyone was well-dressed. The women looked glamorous with their freshly applied makeup and styled hair. From the top floor of the building, we had a three-sixty view of the neighborhood and a breeze!

Our culture has two coffee rituals: the morning coffee ceremony with *manousheh*,[15] and the afternoon one where a variety of desserts, including ice cream, fruits, and pastries, smothered the low coffee table. In many homes, in the center of the coffee table sits an ancient metal serving tray filled with dozens of different brands of cigarettes. This tray symbolizes the extreme generosity Lebanese people pride themselves on. If a visitor wants to smoke, they don't even have to reach for their bag to fetch a cigarette. And if they reach for their bag, they are stopped and strongly encouraged to take a cigarette from the communal tray. This tray is the reason I love cigarettes. During my teen years in Lebanon, I sampled every cigarette brand until I developed an addiction to nicotine. I started smoking in earnest but in secret at sixteen, and shamelessly out in the open, in front of my elders, at seventeen. Young smokers were not discouraged from smoking for too long because every single adult chain smoked.

While my grandmother and the rest of my family were waiting for a neighbor to join them for coffee, my grandfather invited me to join him on the roof—his personal sanctuary, an open-air artist's atelier shaded by gigantic grape leaves that climbed and drooped over trellises. There were sculptures, native plants, and parrots decorating the space. Rain and sun had slowly eroded my grandfather's art, sculptural pieces created with different metals, concrete (he was a great concrete artist), and clay. On that roof I did not receive slaps but important teachings. Knowledge and wisdom I was never taught at school, and quite frankly, knowledge that is purposefully discredited and erased by the Global North.

Much of my grandfather's art and teachings represent relationships in society and are crystalized in certain themes that he shared with me:

Through all our colonization through the centuries, our connection to the soil is our connection to God. He could take the soil of any plant in his palm and from it would sprout another plant. He was gifted with seeds. He would plant all day and tell me sacred stories about our origins. He also saw his connection to the Lebanese soil as going back thousands of years, something I have since verified (as if we needed science to validate it) through a DNA test that I am 99.7% Middle Eastern. He considered that our connection to the land predates all the modern cultures, all the way back to the Phoenicians.

A man is alone, while women are always in community. He saw women at the center of our world and men on the periphery, there to protect the community, especially in the context of war. He shared many stories of survival during the war and hinted at the loneliness he felt while guarding the buildings outside, and I felt the weight of all that he had seen but could not share with me because it was too painful.

We live outside the Colonizers' Way. Our own origin stories are grounded in our perception, language, and culture. They are not the stories told by others who inserted us into their own narratives. Being able to grasp the complexity of various perspectives allowed me to find peace with the fact that I was an outsider, even to my own culture at times.

Science and spirituality are interwoven. Mysticism, poetry, mathematics, astronomy, and science are interconnected in our culture. The separation of science and mysticism resulted in the loss of our sovereignty because it caused us to lose touch with our connection to the Divine.

Nothing is for sure. Unlike the Western belief that cause creates consequences, the Global South's deep understanding of contradiction sees exceptions to the rule and case-by-case situations. Nothing is the same for all of us, and yet, everything can be. There is a lot more nuance to life than narrow-minded man-made laws.

Embrace multiplicity and plurality. Before the first white man came to Beirut, the population that lived there was diverse, and many people held different religious beliefs, came from different tribes and different cultures, and yet were not segregated based on their beliefs or ethnicity. All had a place to exist. There wasn't a need to separate anyone from either nature or each other.

Living Outside the Colonizers' Way

As a teenager coming from Montreal in the Global North, my initial observations when I moved back to Lebanon were tainted by the racism I'd experienced and the education I'd received, which had omitted parts of the world as unknown zones and focused on the conquests and wars won by the Global North. The narrative surrounding "Third World" countries was derogatory and condescending toward the people living here. And the newer "Developing" label is steeped in condescension. It ignores the subjugation and exploitation of the colonized areas by the colonizers. In my education, explanations of global political and economic realities were never tied to colonialism and were presented in a vacuum that disregarded land theft, forced enslavement, and other war tactics European countries used to steal resources, riches, historical artifacts, and other treasures from the countries they ruthlessly colonized.

Because of this, I unconsciously approached my move back to Lebanon from the perspective of the colonizer—not that Canada had colonized Lebanon, but the same Western European powers that had invaded Lebanon a hundred years ago (and a thousand years ago) had colonized Canada and erased, murdered, and tortured the Indigenous populations that lived there. They stole their land and continue to deprive them of their human rights to this day. Canada, just like the United States, has always and continues to violate treaties and invade Indigenous lands to exploit natural resources.

European entitlement has made sure that perspectives outside of their own are automatically discredited. As a survival mechanism, colonized populations may end up assimilating and internalizing this way of life, prioritizing only what is white-centered and disdaining and rejecting their own culture and people. My parents' generation has had severe cases of internalized colonialism, and through the years in Canada my mother would not say where she was from. She would always respond, "We are from Europe," to the question, "Where are you from?" which was asked repeatedly and endlessly. Although of course her response was completely inaccurate, she was only trying to survive in an extremely anti-Arab climate and openly racist culture. Going back to Lebanon allowed me to gain perspective on different world views. It allowed me to expand my thinking and understanding of how the world is perceived and who gets to design it. It also allowed me more empathy for my parents' survival tactics.

My grandfather's teachings gave me permission to be proud of my people and who I am. I gained a sense of agency by better understanding our struggle, our culture, and our creative abilities. It wasn't just learning about the atrocities our people survived, but learning *how* they survived all of it. It was about feeling the strength and pride not just in struggle and survival, but in the joys that remain an inherent part of our lives. How, despite their pain and suffering, they managed to protect their culture and continue to create in a unique way. Gaining this way of looking at the world with a systemic understanding of the context in which everything operates gave me the permission to imagine these systems in a new and different way. The sooner we can gain this powerful perspective, the earlier we can affect change in our lives, even on a systemic level.

Science & Spirituality Are Interwoven

The first time I heard of stories of modern-day miracles was in Lebanon during the afternoon coffee rituals on my grandmother's balcony. I heard stories about people being healed despite their diagnosis, or the Virgin appearing in the fog to save someone's life, or the person who fasted for days and eventually was cured of their disease. Countless stories of the supernatural were part of our everyday lives.

Discussions on spirituality were completely shunned in Canada, mostly because I was surrounded by white folks who had decided that all subjects surrounding the spiritual world were false, dangerous, barbaric, and worthy of nothing but mockery. This was a response to the millennia of abuses suffered in the name of and at the hand of the Catholic Church, but the resulting culture seemed to me barren of hope and wonder.

I have been mocked on many occasions because my parents were praying, or because someone's family was fasting. It was as if their primitive naiveté didn't allow them to know any better. That's how it was perceived by the dominant culture. In Lebanon, however, even in doctor's offices, discussions of God and spirituality happened in a natural way. In our vocabulary, *Inshallah* (God willing), punctuates every other sentence. It carries the sense of "hopefully," although it can also mean, somewhat sarcastically, "This will never happen."

In my grandfather's understanding of scientific knowledge, the spiritual world wasn't tied to religion but to Nature. He knew that the names and cultures that have come in waves are layers on top of each other. Many discoveries made by our ancestors began as an observation of Nature as mystical.

In the hills near Byblos (Jbeil), there is a river valley that springs from what's known as Ishtar's cave at Afqa. Ishtar (or Astarte, later called Aphrodite by the Greeks) fell in love with a boy from Byblos named Adonis and loved him so deeply that Baal became jealous and killed him. This is where his blood flowed and turned the river red. As Ishtar begged Mot, the God of Death, to restore Adonis to life, it was agreed that he could come back each spring and summer, if he returned to the underworld in the fall and winter. We know that when the Adonis River flows from the cave again each spring, the melts bring waters tinted with iron from the mountains. Each fall the flows dry up and leave the valley bare until spring. This story, originating in what is now called Lebanon, has been a core part of spiritual beliefs of cultures from the Greeks to Romans and the story of this river is still alive today, all these thousands of years later.

Most observations on star formations, astronomy, and the direct relationship between the observation of the stars and mathematics also started with an intimate connection to the Divine. Removing the presence of mystery and the desecration of our cultures were tools of oppression that allowed the rulers to better take control of their conquered lands. My philosophy teacher in Beirut told us that colonizers feared two things: love and ideas. Love, because it is a powerful emotion that can turn the subject into a fearless and reckless threat to domination. And ideas, because they come directly from the spiritual world, the plane of creation, unpredictable and extremely convincing. If ideas are shared, they are amplified in intensity and can have the magnitude to move mountains. This is extremely threatening to the ruling power.

In the colonial playbook, along with military might, disempowering people through ideology is the primary method for gaining control and extracting resources. It must be done in such a way that people obey and become easy to subjugate. Lack of access to spirituality, science, and information creates a favorable situation for obedience. This means cutting people off from their ability to read wind patterns, know when the rain will come, and understand the cycles of harvest—all our native ways of understanding Nature, science, and spirituality.

Nothing Is Certain

This doesn't mean we cannot be assertive or have strong convictions about something, or that we cannot control our destinies to a certain extent. This level of understanding allows our minds to remain open to possibilities, to embrace the mystery of life that continues to be present. Living in times of uncertainty evolves our minds to accept the unknown and creatively manage anything that comes our way. This manifests itself in plans not working out and the necessary detachment needed to remain level-headed when something disruptive happens. War and destruction have been a life-altering factor in Lebanon, forever changing both the landscape and human psyches.

Climate change is a direct result of wars, fossil fuel extraction, and greenhouse gas emissions. The land we inhabit has been used as a sacrificial zone, where our way of life has been discredited and where our very lives have been erased for the benefit of the Global North. The fundamental understanding that nothing is quite certain opens a possibility for our sovereignty and gives us permission to imagine new outcomes. In the face of solid conviction, being at ease with uncertainty is a strength. In today's climate chaos era, we are collectively living with the unknown. The main dialogue in the climate justice space has been primarily delivered by white-bodied individuals, often men, who claim with utter certainty that we are doomed to burn in hell right here on this planet. This is said without the acknowledgment that the imminent hell on earth they predict is a result of the destruction that their own colonial industrialized cultures have made.

It's absolutely jarring to hear and enough of an apocalyptic depiction to throw anyone who has survived a war into CPTSD[16] when reading about climate predictions. For communities living in red zones,[17] climate change is already part of their everyday struggle. For instance, in Lebanon, not having access to drinking water, electricity, and fuel are all a direct consequence of climate change. Even with this level of tragedy and chaos, culturally we prepare ourselves for whatever outcomes may happen. Living in survival mode in this way takes a toll on our mental and physical health. The key is to know that no matter how things may seem to be set in stone, nothing is for sure—and therefore there is always an unexpected way.

Embracing Multiplicity & Plurality

In Lebanon, there is no single, simple ethnicity. We aren't a people that share the same ethnic makeup throughout our lands. Our skin color varies from dark brown to fair with red hair and blue eyes. All the port cities (Tripoli, Byblos, Beirut, Tyre, and Sidon) were entry points for peoples of the Mediterranean. They were hubs of culture and knowledge, and the area was one of the cradles of civilization. We built boats made of cedar wood and traveled the world. Remains of our ancestors were found in grottos in Italy, Spain, Portugal, Greece, Morocco, Algeria, Tunisia, and Libya. There was a further alliance with the adoption of Arabic across the region. In more modern times, the Levant region was connected by rail, from Damascus to Cairo by way of Beirut and Jerusalem.

Education has always been regarded as a higher form of connection with the Divine and was also considered a human right long before the West adopted these values. In the region alone there are more than fifteen different religions. Although the region was often subject to attacks and occupations notably by the Ottoman Empire before the French and English came to occupy the area, there were long eras of peace where our people prospered, created art, and shared knowledge in order to advance our humanity. The largest libraries were located in SWANA: Southwest Asia and North Africa, or the Middle East.[18]

Listening to stories told by family and friends that highlight our shared history always inspires me deeply. Just like my grandfather, I always was attracted to the field of education. Learning is truly a gift. Being able to expand our knowledge as well as the dimensions of reality has changed my life. Knowledge has been a form of refuge for me throughout my life. Learning and unlearning are liberatory work. In that spirit I've always embraced plurality.

As a first-generation war survivor, I don't have it in me to promote division and hatred. Near-death experiences sharpened my senses to be aware of death and to also see the immenseness of life. I am constantly guided by this sense of pluriversal diplomacy and democracy. It gave me the certainty and urge at times to praise equality, often in the school courtyard while all were openly debating human rights, political education, and history. I stepped in to share that we have lived in a time where Jews, Christians, Muslims, Druze, Baha'i, and many other religious groups coexisted in peace and harmony. When challenged about this idea with "Muslims will kill all the Christians," or "No, the Christians murdered all the Muslims," I responded, "I love Muslims, Christians, Jews, and all people and hope we get to know what it's like to live in peace on this land!"

The word *land* had barely been pronounced when, unexpectedly, a massive *SLAP!* resonated in my ears. My cheek started pounding, almost pulsating, my body temperature rose then dropped. I was in a state of shock. Looking around, people started to gather. My hand remained on my cheek, right where I had received the slap.

NOTES

9. Mazars are small altars, often at roadsides with small statues of saints, Mary, or other Christian figures.

10. Kaak is a type of sesame-covered street bread.

11. Jeddo is Arabic for "grandfather."

12. Habibi is a common term of endearment meaning "beloved."

13. Ahlan is "Welcome" in Arabic.

14. Ya Ahla w Sahla is "Welcome!"

15. Manousheh is a traditional flatbread.

16. Complex post-traumatic stress disorder (complex PTSD, sometimes abbreviated to c-PTSD or CPTSD) is a condition where you experience some symptoms of PTSD along with additional symptoms, such as difficulty controlling your emotions, feeling very angry or distrustful toward the world.

17. Red Zones refer to an IPCC report: "Code red" for human-driven global heating. A United Nations official warns that in the coming decades climate changes will increase in all regions.

18. Some argue that the appellation of the region as "Middle East" is a colonial adoption as it is in relationship to Europe. In fact, that isn't accurate since it is unclear what Middle or East represent in this case. Southwest Asia and North Africa or SWANA is a new term, at first contested and later on adopted to refer to the geographic region of Occupied Palestine, Türkiye, Lebanon, Syria, Jordan, Iraq, Egypt, Cyprus, Libya, Saudi Arabia, Oman, Yemen, Bahrain, Armenia, Azerbaijan, Kuwait, Qatar, and UAE.

CHAPTER VI

Fashion
&
Politics

Cassette #6: "Gangsta's Paradise"

Coolio blasts into my Walkman on loop. I'm getting dressed in front of the small mirror in my auntie's childhood bedroom, looking at my reflection, trying to know who I am. It seems like I'm looking at a stranger in the small mirrors with hand-painted depictions of Mickey Mouse and Donald Duck. From the next room I can hear "Shik Shak Shok" by Hassan Abu El Seoud, contrasting with what is playing on my Walkman.

This chapter could be a book in itself. In fact, before embarking on *A Woman Is a School*, I considered writing a book on Fashion Colonialism. Instead, I opted to build an open library and curriculum around that topic and to dedicate my first book to systems of knowledge that are often both discredited and endangered. In mapping Fashion systems, I discovered that the model looks like a vacuum, on the one end sucking up resources, and on the other outputting waste. Systems are designed to be invisible; they only become apparent to us when they break (climate change), when they don't work in our favor (racial injustice), and when they harm us (policing, prisons, wars, military occupation).

The complexity and compounding issues and data points make it extremely difficult for people to understand or to articulate precisely what needs to change in a given oppressive system. Part of systemic change is the creation of language and awareness around naming the harm. Many have built extensive careers in "naming the harm," where their business models may hinder the solutions of the harm they so passionately stand against.

For instance, someone advocating for fair fashion systems by only naming the harm and not participating in creating alternative solutions may be reluctant to change. Systemic change requires us to change. This also means our business models tied to the work of transformation must be designed to evolve throughout the different phases of change. The second part of systemic change is radically healing before we embark on radical imagination. In the healing process, after we've named the harm, we explore strategies of care and frameworks of collective healing that may resemble the kitchen table makeup classes my auntie Nona used to host. In community, we gather, communicate our grievances, unlearn and learn new ways of addressing issues, and connect together. Community is sacred, a healing place.

We arrived in Beirut in the summer of 1996. It was unusually hot, and the heat and humidity were paralyzing. I asked myself time and again how my parents could have left a country where they had a home, a job, and safety. How could they have thrown that all in the air to return to postapocalyptic Beirut?

People in Beirut were dressed as if they were stuck in a time capsule from the '70s. Everyone wore classic European styles with traditional Lebanese, Syrian, and Palestinian accents. Wooden Scholl clogs with perfectly painted red toes, shorts made of flowered fabric, bras that turned breasts into two perfect ice-cream cones peeking through poplin cotton tops. All the women had perfectly dyed and straightened hair set with tons of hairspray by local hairdressers.

My long curly hair was difficult to brush, and I didn't have access to good styling products. I generally chose to wear it in a bun, leaving two strands of hair hanging on either side of my face. I cherished the items I'd brought with me from Montreal: crop tops, baggy jeans, and chunky sneakers.

When we arrived, we were reintroduced to family members—cousins, aunties, and grandparents who we had not had the chance to know. They were so generous, kind, and passionately welcoming. They looked at us as though we were long lost siblings. The reunions were loud and teary; wet kisses and long uncomfortable hugs were given. Our extended family was eager to create stronger bonds with us to make up for lost time. We were invited to every family function: long lunches at restaurants somewhere far away in the pristine mountains, coffee ceremonies at different relatives' houses. We could spend the entire day at various coffee ceremonies. Of course, the ultimate invitation was to accompany some long lost relative to hang out on the beach for long days in the sun. I swam in the Mediterranean water for hours. I would have lapped up that water if I could have.

This magical time was a prolonged celebration, an antidote to living through decades of war. After the cease-fire was declared, flocks of Lebanese immigrants rushed back into their country to rebuild. They were now the expats—a class of their own, coming back home with hard-earned wealth and ideas about how to modernize their war-torn country.

In every restaurant we went to, Arabic music played loudly from low-fi speakers; an upbeat, energizing new wave of pop songs replaced the melancholic nostalgic sounds of Fairuz and got people off their chairs in the middle of lunch to spontaneously start dancing. They would pull their family members onto their feet and create large circles of chaos and celebration. It is very common in Lebanon to interrupt a long Sunday lunch to dance near the tables, or further away in the center of the place, making a beautiful spectacle of joy. Nothing was like the postwar Lebanon era, when the dancing began at lunchtime and continued in the nightclubs until the sun rose the next morning. Nightclub scenes welcomed everyone of all ages. As a fourteen-year-old, I got the chance to witness Beirut's nightlife. Dancing on rooftops, dancing on bars, getting wasted on cigarettes and alcohol, to then wake up for a Sunday lunch that spanned over four hours from two in the afternoon until six in the evening. These "lunches" were interspersed with dancing, cigarettes, and *arguilé* (the *shisha* or hooka) smoking, and long conversations about our very promising future. That was the culture I was falling in love with. During these long Sunday lunches, there was one song in particular that summarizes that time and that would most definitely get the entire restaurant up on their feet dancing together with family and strangers—"Raje3 Yet3amar Lebnan," راجـع يتعمـر لبنـان , by Zaki Nassif. The song translates to "Lebanon will be rebuilt," or "We are rebuilding Lebanon ... it will be greener than ever, back to our roots, back to our land."

It's a powerful anthem that, given the failed state Lebanon was in, had a nostalgic message and inspired a dream to re-create a life that would refute the apocalyptic scenarios people had survived and the bleak anticipation of political unrest we were all dreading—and that sadly proved to be inevitable. I kept asking my parents if there was going to be another war in Lebanon, and they would answer with confidence, "No! There will be no more war! Nobody wants a war!" I often asked that question as Israeli war planes flew low over Beirut breaking the sound barrier and creating a deafening, explosive boom!

My first perception of this song and the Lebanese era I was parachuted into was clouded by my own teenage angst and the loss I was experiencing at having been uprooted once again from what I thought was my life, my identity. The disdain I was experiencing was overwhelming. At that time I started reading Camus's *L'Étranger* and related on a visceral level to the contempt the main character felt for his circumstances. Little did I know that I had been indoctrinated to believe Western paradigms of superiority and power over my own lived experience and traditional knowledge systems. I had become a critic of my own culture. I had aligned myself with the whiteness of being and believed that the Europeans who have colonized Turtle Island—so-called Canada and the United States—were right to do so because they had created "progress" and "improved" the circumstances of their subordinates. I was fed this doctrine at school, and although I lived in a liberal and somewhat progressive city, Montreal, the general sentiment was that European blood, ideas, and methods were superior, no questions asked, to any other culture or people on this planet. I had unconsciously adopted the "white gaze" and trained it on my own people and myself. That misunderstanding, along with the general obnoxious attitude I, as a teenager, had toward just about anything, was undoubtedly the main reason for my misery.

Although I had the opportunity to witness my country rise from its own ashes and blood, I had this overpowering critical voice in my head narrating the situation complicated with layers of nihilism and despair. No matter what was in front of me—a bowl of fruit, a platter of sweets, the Mediterranean beach—it was perceived with disdain borrowed from my favorite white male authors' words. Their words and the education I'd received in the Global North made me certain that no matter how much of a miracle I was witnessing, the truth was bleak. I recognized this inner critic in most of my peers, a sort of unconscious "frenemy" we adopted and believed over the reality of our own senses. A voice that can suck the life out of anything real and choke joy with despair. An eternal sense of doom that seems to convey reality.

My parents were inspired and encouraged to explore new ways of contributing to their country. The song in the restaurant wasn't just an anthem, it was a call to action.

Every Lebanese of their generation wanted to bring a piece of the West back into their country. Some opened burger joints and called them silly American names; others opened pizza parlors and claimed to have the best pizza. Others, more ambitious, opened franchises such as Pizza Hut or McDonald's. But these franchises took years to solidify. My parents were both employed by two separate companies, one solving the waste crisis in Lebanon and the other importing European clothes to the Middle East. In hindsight, both of their career paths have inspired my own. My focus on waste in the fashion industry and how the rise of fast fashion in our country has impacted our culture are core arteries of my work at Slow Factory.

My father took on an executive position in the financial department at Sukleen, a waste management company in Lebanon. The company had more problems than solutions for the growing waste issue inherited from nearby countries. During the war, European countries as well as Israel used Lebanon as their proxy landfill and sent out boatloads of garbage that were dumped on our shores.[19] We continue to witness this "waste colonialism" today with textile waste from countries of the Global North off-loaded onto the shores of countries of the Global South, including Ghana, Chile, Vietnam, and Pakistan. The waste Lebanon received was highly toxic and severely polluted our water, soil, and air. I encouraged my father to get his company to consider recycling, but unfortunately, he seemed to be uninterested in exploring something as "mundane" as recycling.

My mother began working at a fashion company that imported European brands to Lebanon. Her work with this company inspired her to start her own fashion business by importing plus-size clothing to Lebanon, which would allow women who weren't a small European size to enjoy elegant modern fashion. Scrap the abaya for a skirt suit—known as a *tailleur* in French. This skirt suit borrowed from French fashion ultimately became a much-in-demand Lebanese staple. Before my mother embarked on her own entrepreneurial journey, she helped many women in Lebanon import clothing from Türkiye, Romania, France, and Greece to sell independently to their growing clientele. She championed her peers and became herself one of their most enthusiastic customers.

One of the women my mother championed was Latifeh, whose apartment served as a boutique. She stocked hundreds of styles of *tailleur* for women who weren't small. My mother loved to go to her house and was a frequent customer. I went with her regularly and though my mother was trained as a seamstress—not as a profession but as part of our culture in which every woman must know how to alter clothing—she also had a network of seamstresses ready to alter just about anything to make it fit your body and conform to the trends of the day. A skirt would be altered to be mini but done in a way that when the mini-skirt lifespan ended, it could be altered back to be a midi-skirt—the fabric being tucked in such a way that it could be done and undone. Such was my mother's vision.

I was invited to try on some of the trends that Latifeh scored abroad, but I hated them with my entire being. Every single style reinforced heteropatriarchy. My soul rejected everything they tried to style me with. I refused to wear most of what Latifeh bought for teenagers like me. I wanted something simple, intellectual. I wanted to wear only black. Something like a suit with pants, not a skirt perhaps, even though I was only a young teen. Without my realizing it, my entire idea of womanhood revolved around queer and lesbian fashion. I liked boys' clothes and lingerie. I did not want any froufrou decoration on me. All I wanted Latifeh to bring me back from abroad were running shoes. It seemed that young people in Lebanon did not yet appreciate streetwear. I don't blame them, the fashion capsule we were living in was from a particular era.

Everyone wore Italian-style dress shoes or espadrilles to the beach. I lusted over leather and plastic sneakers, but the Lebanese youth weren't interested in them. Dr. Martens were big in my school at some point; the leather European military-style boots were the shoe of choice to wear with our school uniforms. I begged Latifeh to buy me Dr. Martens, which she did, from Türkiye. Except they were Misses Martens or something like that, a counterfeit copy of the original. I was devastated to realize I'd been duped.

My mother had a mission: to empower the Plus-size Lebanese woman as a Fashionista. However, she despised the fact that my body had changed, and that I had become a fat teenager overwhelmed by depression and anger. During the many trips to Latifeh's home store, I tried to squeeze into pants while crying and feeling hideous, like a monster out of an Alice-in-Wonderland turned horror movie. Picture a woman turned into a giant marshmallow melting out of her own body. I felt ugly, desperate, and lost, hiding in what was now my new room that I shared with my siblings in my grandfather's building, where we now lived. My Walkman on blast, playing Pink Floyd's "Hey You," tears falling, and the sense of complete desolation. I didn't fit anywhere. I had imagined, planned, and organized my own death many times.

I couldn't bear the contrast of my mundane life with the impoverished lives of so many Lebanese I was now in contact with. I was always asking, "What can be done?" Going into politics was discouraged as everyone who attempted to get elected was killed, and then rendered a martyr. We were living in a chaotic country that couldn't provide water or electricity to its citizens, rich or poor. The absurdity of our situation was expressed most clearly by the kids living in the streets who were wearing Adidas and Nike T-shirts and pants. The famous three stripes paired with the *shahata*, the rubber slip-on shoe many Arab comedians joke about as a weapon their parents used to beat them. Humor in our situation was an antidote to pain. Arguably, so was and is fashion.

On my sixteenth birthday in 1998, Zara opened its doors in Beirut, the first fast-fashion retailer to open in Lebanon. Young women from across the country flocked to the store, ready to purchase a piece of European fashion. Fast fashion has the reputation for being cheap and affordable. For us, Zara was expensive but cheap in terms of quality. We were used to locally made, Eastern European independent fashion that Latifeh and others like her imported to the country: high-quality garments durable enough to withstand multiple rounds of alterations, depending on the trends.

"Polyester? *Tsk tsk tsk*," my mother muttered as she touched the fabric of a mini-skirt I desperately wanted. Mini-skirt—I know, so feminine, unlike what I was interested in, but the way I wanted to style it, with my Dr. Martens look-alikes and a crop top, reflected the rebellious sexual energy I was starting to embody. "No, this will make you look fat," my mother said firmly, returning the polyester skirt to the rack.

We shopped for hours and observed that some women had grabbed hundreds of items while others clutched only the one piece they could afford from this fancy store.

Zara in Lebanon was the symbol of what I now know is Fashion and Colonialism. With its arrival, Latifeh's business suffered greatly; most of her clientele wanted the knock-offs and the immediate satisfaction of being in a big store that catered to their European aspirations. Most of them were of my parents' generation and were indoctrinated to loathe their own culture and aspire to be more ... European ... more white. I eventually got a gray mini-skirt with an aubergine twin set, and acrylic tank top with an acrylic cardigan. My mom and I shared the philosophy that everything you buy must be versatile enough to be worn on multiple occasions and for various events and functions.

We thought of Zara as luxury; fast fashion felt luxurious to some of us. Even though the fabric and finishing may not have been the best quality, especially in comparison with Latifeh's finds, it was the brand and style that made us feel like we were part of their world in a way. Most women around me wanted to feel modern, sophisticated, and cool. For those aged sixteen like me, fashion became almost a sacred rite of passage—secretly getting multiple piercings and tattoos to go with our Zara outfits, dressing for the dreams we were becoming. When hitting the streets to protest, my friends and I would wear matching outfits to make an impact. I didn't have much, but I learned how to style efficiently and stick to a style or look that represented me.

I incorporated traditional accents and accessories with the simple modern looks I favored. In the Beirut souks I bought vintage silver jewelry: earrings, necklaces, and broken bits and pieces. Then I would create my own jewelry. I purchased traditional scarves, keffiyehs, and shoes and sandals made in Lebanon or the region. My grandfather Labib had treasures nobody knew about but me. He would open a bag filled with ancient jewelry made of silver and stones and I was allowed to select a few pieces. I still have these pieces to this day and have worn them proudly, my precious luxurious pieces, filled with ancient stories.

There comes a time in every woman's life where the first memory of fashion and identity is tied to a lived experience in which she becomes aware that her body is politicized and that what she wears will dictate how society will perceive her. Throughout my life I have been exposed to fashion through the lens of my mother and aunts who were Lebanese fashion icons in their own right. I learned how to draw the perfect line with eyeliner, a Lebanese style that has inspired fashionable women around the world. I was given *kohl*, a black waxlike cone that women use to draw lines around their eyes. I loved the effect it had on my eyes; I immediately looked and felt connected to my culture. Kohl was my must-have when I was a teen and continues to be my personal signature.

The first time I was made aware of the science behind applying eyeliner was when we were growing up in Montreal in the '90s. My aunt Mona, whom we call Nona, was living with us. She was a talented aesthetician and makeup artist in Beirut. When she moved to Montreal during the war, she went back to school to become an optometrist. But, in the afternoon, Nona hosted circles of women in our kitchen and gave them tutorials on how to anoint themselves like we did back home. Eyeliner, mascara, eyelash curler, eye shadows of various shades, and concealer were displayed on the table, with a medium-sized mirror placed in the center. Nona would demonstrate how to draw the perfect line on one of her friends' eyes, how to extend the eye by brushing the eyebrows upward using a small brush, and how to create an illusion of light by applying a line of concealer just under the eyebrow, right where the hair stops. She taught how to use the different shades of eye shadow to create the signature Lebanese smoky eyes to give a look and attitude of royalty, elegance, and mystery.

Every time I trace my own eyeliner over my eyelids, different stories come to me. In 2016 I filmed a short documentary in Beddawi Refugee Camp. It was a project I undertook with Slow Factory as part of our humanitarian work to break the cycle of "poverty porn" being presented to us about refugees in Lebanon. The film focused the free skills training programs that ANERA (American Near East Refugee Aid) provided for refugees in Lebanon. Our crew was composed of my husband Colin, my sister Laeticia, my dear friend Hady (who once was my math tutor when I was sixteen), and our filmmaker friend Rami.

Beddawi Camp is one of the oldest and most densely populated refugee camps in Lebanon. The refugees were of course from the Nakba, the catastrophe of the creation of the state of Israel in historic Palestine. At the time there had been there had been a new influx of refugees from Syria to escape the destruction there.

As we entered the camp, we realized it was a city within a city with street names, alleyways, a broken amusement park the United Nations had once built, and the smell of fresh laundry and food cooking. There was a square where everyone would hang out, complete with shops selling knockoff Adidas, Nike, and other American brands. The camp was established by UNRWA (United Nations

Relief and Works Agency) in 1955 as the first flow of refugees came fleeing the Israeli annexation of Palestine. Though only one square kilometer, it is a functional city of almost 20,000 people. Houses, roads, a makeshift electrical grid, and infrastructure have all sprouted up and evolved over the years with little help from the municipalities outside the walls. Entire generations have been raised in the enclosure, without rights to citizenship or work in their country of refuge, Lebanon.

We parked our car next to a broken-down, rusty Ferris wheel, probably installed by an international NGO (non-governmental organization) for refugee children during some earlier epoch. Our first stop was the job-training school run by ANERA. "Beauty and makeup class is one of our most popular courses in the program," said Maggie Forster, ANERA's vice president for philanthropy and our point of contact there.

This trip confirmed for me that fashion was used as a coping mechanism in our culture. We were welcomed by Samara Khalife, a Palestinian refugee who ran a beauty parlor in the camp that also happened to be one of the most coveted and in-demand beauty salons in the area (inside and outside the camp). She looked at me with the same disapproving face my mother made when she saw me without makeup on, dressed down in denim like an American who doesn't care.

She said, "Habibti, come sit in my chair."

She began gently tilting my head back and applying eyeliner to my closed eyelids. I completely surrendered, resting my head on the chair supported by her soft hands, while the eyeliner's cool ink slowly dried on my eyelids. When she finished, she helped me sit up straight and applied mascara on my lashes. When she was finished, she exclaimed, "This is how you show up, always your best self."

In 1986 when we were forced to flee Lebanon as refugees, my mother, who had a serious makeup routine, considered the morning of our departure to be no exception. Despite our need to leave immediately, she applied her signature Lebanese kohl eyeliner and carefully contoured her lips with lip pencil before swiping on lipstick. This makeup style was de rigueur in the early '80s, as was her big hair. We children (both under five years old) were wearing our Sunday best.

Arriving at our destination, my mother, a twenty-year-old Beiruti with two young children, had to figure out her way around the West. Fashion had always been her armor and her protection, but she stood out, and not in a way she was comfortable with. Winters in Montreal are particularly difficult, especially for someone who's never experienced any temperature below freezing. To dress for temperatures that reach below minus 35 degrees Celsius (minus 31 degrees Fahrenheit) was in itself a traumatic experience.

Not to diminish my mother's *real* trauma: learning to dress for Canadian winters without losing herself, her style, and her connection to her culture proved to be a journey of self-exploration and defiance. For example, she would refuse to wear flat boots or shapeless, nonfeminine coats. She insisted on walking on ice in heels, and rather than practical ski mittens, wore thin, chic leather gloves and a form-fitting Lebanese coat. She refused to wear a winter hat (a *toque* in Canada) that might mash her big hair, and insisted on her signature black eyeliner, though her eyes would tear up from the glacial wind and black streaks would line her face. The leather gloves barely prevented frostbite, and she was always in danger of losing her footing on the ice. She was battling assimilation, the pressure to fit in as part of this new world. This melting pot, as it was called in the '80s and '90s in Canada, this drive to create a homogenous and universal people is a symptom of colonialism. So many immigrants and refugees are asked to shed their culture as a "respectable" way to accept shelter in the West. Fashion becomes political as soon as they land.

A Middle Eastern woman—who has grown to believe she is proudly from the "Paris of the Middle East" as the saying goes when describing Beirut, especially before the 1975 war—always sees fashion as a political tool for informing her community on her status, her style, and her religious beliefs. In Lebanon, women are raised to show up in their communities impeccably dressed, with every hair in place whether worn in the hijab or "properly" westernized by the local hairdresser. Eyeliner and contoured lips must be perfect, and an additional mole might be drawn next to the lip to add drama. Under colonial rule in Lebanon, fashion, culture, and agriculture were deeply affected by European values. Women's bodies became sites of struggle between two cultures. Fashion has been, over the past hundred years, a visible reflection of the colonial wars where our traditional clothes have been cast as less evolved, less modern, and of lesser value than European fashion. Women choosing to wear our traditional clothes were portrayed as peasants—ignorant, barbaric, and less evolved than the European settlers sourcing their silks from the Lebanese mountains.

This notion that all people should be one thing is absurd and impossible, yet we continue to push forward initiatives and narratives born of this failed premise. Pluralism is the political philosophy holding that people of different beliefs, backgrounds, and lifestyles can coexist in the same society and participate equally in the political process. Climate disaster, colonial expansion, military occupation, and wars impact our natural habitat but also our collective knowledge. National and personal archives, libraries, photo studios, and museums have been pillaged, burned down, and destroyed. Most of our artifacts are in museums around the world. We in Lebanon are subject to collective amnesia when it comes to our history, identity, and native wisdom. Yet, through our fashions, there are clues that are left for us to interpret and to remind us of our stories.

The region we now call Lebanon was an area that has been interacting with colonizers and occupiers for thousands of years. Different conquering cultures approach interaction with the conquered lands and people in different ways. Europeans have been drawn in waves to the "cradle of civilization," as the region has been called. Early Europeans marveled at our diverse and unusual culture where differences were accepted and celebrated. Alexander the Great, the ancient Greek king of Macedonia, was a proponent of the idea of universalism. As a leader he would encourage his men to interact with the local folks, and on many occasions, even allow them to take wives from these local tribes as their own. The Greeks, however, despite adopting some of the languages and clothing and this exchange of culture and fashion, maintained that they were the superior race.

It is said that when the Romans occupied Lebanon, they borrowed traditions and local fashion to blend in with the occupied peoples. They often learned the language and espoused the culture they colonized. That was a peace mechanism designed to create a universal aesthetic and culture. Universalism is a concept later adopted by the Christian Church when it expanded its colonial dominance in the world. However, the Church used universalism as a way to "educate" the native people it subjugated by criminalizing their fashion and religious symbols and erasing their history, culture, fashion, and habits. The Church propagated the idea that they were "modernizing" native people around the world. Modernism, as the basis of colonial dominance, has contributed to the almost total erasure of the plurality of different ethnic and native groups and identities around the world. Fashion, politics, and modernism are somewhat intertwined.

Universalism is a school of thought in Christian theology that focuses on the doctrine of universal reconciliation, or the view that all human beings will ultimately be saved and restored with a right relationship to God. History shows how violently this has been interpreted and how reconciliation was used to spread colonialism and the power of some of these empires. As we battle the monocultures colonialism has produced (monocultures in both agriculture and culture), some of us have embarked on a quest to trace our origins, identity, and traditional knowledge systems.

Every trip back to Lebanon, I ask my elders, the ones who are still with us, to tell me their stories: "What was it like before? What did you do to look beautiful, Téta[20]?"

Téta Souad responds, "I washed my face with traditional soap and put almond oil all over my body and hair."

My quest to discover "what it was like before" extends beyond beauty routines. It is about retrieving lost information that can illuminate more about who we were and how; by connecting with our past, we can move forward toward collective liberation and healing. What does fashion have to do with this, you may ask? Fashion creates meaning, and meaning can inspire action. *Fashion Activism* is a term I define as the act of using fashion as a platform for social and environmental change.

Fashion, Sustainability & Colonialism

Fashion is a powerful industry and is said to be responsible for 8–10 percent of all global carbon emissions. Through our consumption of fashion, we produce, purchase, are exposed to, and throw away hundreds of thousands of microplastics produced by polyester fabrics. The clothes we wear that are manufactured and sold by the fast-fashion industries are largely made with fossil fuel fabrics and toxic dyes that are destroying our rivers and streams. In addition, these clothes are often made by women living below the poverty line in dreadful circumstances. Universalism and oppressive aesthetics are forced on populations by the overproduction of and easy access to products produced by colonial culture—a culture of ease that promises a path to wealth and power.

Throughout my work I have advocated for sustainable practices in fashion and have provided solutions for ethical manufacturing and material production. My work has been published on international media platforms, and in journals, magazines, and academic journals, yet much of it has been plagiarized in books (without citation) created after those writing the books attended my lectures, classes, and workshops.

In 2018 I created a comprehensive map tracing supply chains for most of our daily goods related to the fashion and beauty industries. The routes' map is identical to colonial routes predating our current economic reality by five hundred years. Colonialism is not a thing of the past; it is a current economic reality. In my class

"Fashion & Colonialism," I dive deeper into what universalism is in relation to fashion and how this idea is used as an oppressive tool for control and domination. Take, for instance, the debate about the burqa in France. Is it oppressive to wear the burqa in public? Or is it oppressive to force women not to wear it against their will? How has modernity defined our freedom as women, and where does it contradict our own decisions for our own safety and sense of self?

The notion that modern is better than the old means that the old becomes obsolete and soon waste in a landfill unless someone finds value in the old thing. When we are experiencing a constant feed of what modernity, beauty, wealth, and fashion is, that feed begins to obscure the erasure of our cultures, identities, and traditions. What does fashion mean to you? What makes you feel unique, comfortable, and at ease? This may be a kaftan or abaya dress; this may mean being nude all day. The point is to redefine what fashion means on a personal level before seeking to achieve unattainable goals designed to make us feel incomplete and undesirable. In Latifeh's shop, women shared stories. The experience was less about purchasing a new *tailleur*, and more about playing dress-up, being in community, and being seen and heard. Fashion is not only a coping mechanism; it is medicine.

During one of my recent visits to the National Museum of Lebanon (El Mathaf), I was admiring the collection of jewels and a small selection of embroideries used on dresses and headpieces. As I was admiring the collection, the electricity went out, a normal occurrence in Lebanon. It happened in grocery stores, at the hairdresser's, in the mall, and even at Zara. Power cuts occurred at least five times per day and always took a few minutes to be restored by a generator.

While the electricity was out in the museum, we were submerged in the dark for a few minutes. I turned on the flashlight feature on my phone to locate my children and my partner. Once I found them, we began exploring the collection in the dark with the flashlight on. The generator took more than ten minutes to restore the electricity, so our visit to the museum felt like we were in a cave we had uncovered, looking at precious artifacts through the gleam of the flashlight. What was remarkable about observing our ancestors' jewelry and fashion in this way was realizing the symbolism and our spiritual connection to each piece. Embroideries told stories, jewelry held protective and magical powers. Nothing was worn with empty meaning. Everything had a dense aura of symbolism, art, and spirituality.

What has happened that we now walk around in a dangerous yet fascinating world without our protections, talismans, or embroideries made by women in a village praying and infusing garments with spirit? The desanctification of our native cultures is part of the colonial playbook applied unilaterally throughout the globe. When talking with my dear friend Charles al-Hayek about the first contact our ancestors in Lebanon had with Europeans, he had a hard time pinpointing it. Unlike the clear "discovery" of the Americas, Beirut was a port, strategically positioned between East and West, and continually discovered, so to speak, since antiquity. However, in our scriptures there are observations of Europeans, particularly French and English travelers in the 1800s during the Ottoman Empire, who marveled that—in Beirut particularly but valid for most of Lebanon—folks were dressed in ways that didn't reveal their religious identities.

Christian, Muslim, Druze, Buddhist, Baha'i—no matter the religious faith, folks were dressed following diverse yet similar aesthetics and traditions: the sherwal, the abaya, the headwraps, the tantour, the tarbush, were items worn by all. The Europeans marveled at the unity between cultures, and although a Bedouin was recognizably different than a clerk working for a city leader or a European dressed in a suit, acceptance was the norm. A form of "live and let live" had been adopted at that time, which was arguably one of the most peaceful eras in the region.

However, peace doesn't equate with justice; peace just means it was a time without conflict and war. According to Charles al-Hayek, Europeans were instrumental in breaking the solidarity between different ethnic groups that made up the Lebanese community. They began to create false hierarchies by becoming closer to the Christian Maronites, and by default separating them from their fellow Muslims. They did this first through fashion by introducing the idea of modernity. The suit, for instance, became an expression of aristocracy and contributed to the idea of the "elevated man"—the start of the separation of our nation.

Fashion & Waste

Fashion waste is not really waste, it is simply unused resources. Sadly, both waste that could be reused and waste that has been created without the reasonable possibility of reuse all end up in the landfills. When I sat down to connect the dots in my life and find my way amidst a career change and a new child in 2012, I wanted to work with the concept of Slow Factory that my partner and I had conceptualized years before in 2008. Having given birth to our first daughter, Sila Grey, we returned to Beirut for a year so I could reconnect with myself and be surrounded by my family. My husband, who is Canadian, wanted to learn Arabic so he could communicate with my grandfather. While in Lebanon, I started sketching ideas in a notebook. At the time my father was still consulting with the waste management company in Lebanon, and my mother was running her business importing clothes of all sizes (especially plus sizes) to the Middle East.

The waste crisis in Lebanon is ongoing. I couldn't help but notice and smell—and feel an endless sense of despair, the same one I had felt as a teenager witnessing a failed system. What could we do? How could we solve the waste problem, not only in Lebanon, but everywhere? In my notebook I began writing about my interest in solving the waste problem and pollution in general. I was concerned about the chemicals used in most of our products—identity and styles that fade in and out of fashion. I used skills that I had been taught in Paris by Patrick André depuis 1966: conceptualizing concepts. This sounds redundant, but it is the act of birthing ideas.

I began writing about what I knew: design, data analysis, information architecture, art, and culture. And I continued to focus on issues I was passionate about: human rights, the refugee crisis, systemic improvements, and change. Soon the notebook looked like a constellation of random focus points. I do have an attention deficit disorder and am hyperactive; maybe my notebook was just a representation of the incompetencies of my brain? Perhaps I am unable to make sense of what appears to be chaotic and random. Just like any of the sensemaking jobs I was presented with throughout my career, I began drawing lines between points and building a bridge of understanding between, for example, fashion and waste.

I looked at my mother's and father's jobs and how the two are interconnected. Through this exercise the birth of Slow Factory began—an organization that would use fashion as a medium for social and environmental change. Fashion, as a utilitarian art form, impacts everyone. Walking naked has for many ended in police custody, even in the most liberal countries. Clothing is a second skin. However, as much as we can shed skin and transform to become our full complex selves, we can never justify the churn of textile waste emitted by the ton from the Global North and dumped in the Global South.

People often ask: "What can I do?" And bloggers, TikTokers, and Instagrammers respond: "Buy less, choose well," a sentence borrowed from Vivienne Westwood who encouraged us to mend and care for our clothes rather than purchasing mindlessly or buying in bulk and then throwing half of our purchases out in donation bins. The body of work I created for Open Education as part of Slow Factory's free climate education program elaborates on issues tied to the fashion industry, including waste, forced labor, and toxic chemical usage in most of our clothing, and offers systemic rather than Band-Aid solutions. Systemic solutions tackle the very system that is designed to extract and pollute. Band-Aid solutions produce slogans such as "Boycott Fast Fashion," "Buy secondhand clothing only," and "Eat vegan food." These slogans aren't completely useless, but they are not absolutes. We must use our collective imagination to design new systems as well as reimagine and innovate structures of production that lead to regenerative outcomes such as waste-to-resource production, community-centered models of creation, and profit sharing.

Below I am including a few models: one in naming the harm and proposing a new avenue, and the other about frameworks of collective healing that I have developed as part of a retreat by RISD (Rhode Island School of Design) Center for Complexity I was invited to attend while writing this book. Both are mapping systems and provide open frameworks of transformation and care. These are the models we are exploring within the fashion industry and beyond, as Slow Factory's work acts as a connective tissue across all industries and sectors.

This approach is borrowed from cultures of the Global South, particularly my Lebanese upbringing and ancestry: circular interconnected models built, not like vacuums, but like spirals. The very concept of Fashion & Politics was labeled "far-fetched" when I developed it in 2013. Seeing interconnectedness is a skill that is taught within our Open Education Program, and is, interestingly, a skill that is innate for those of us who are born and raised in the cultures of the Global South. Our traditional wisdom is generously taught to us through various formats: stories, our survival of collective trauma, slaps on our faces, love stories, coffee ceremonies, and our ability to discern and observe.

**Framework for
collective healing**

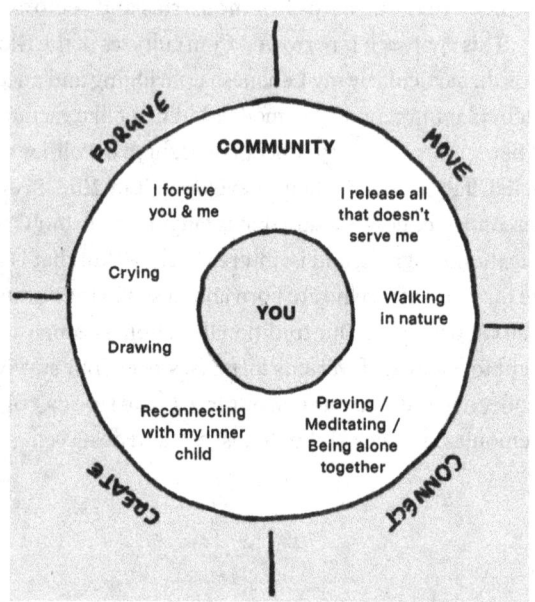

Systems Literacy
From <u>waste</u> to <u>resource</u>

● Current systems based on extraction
◐ New systems based on regeneration

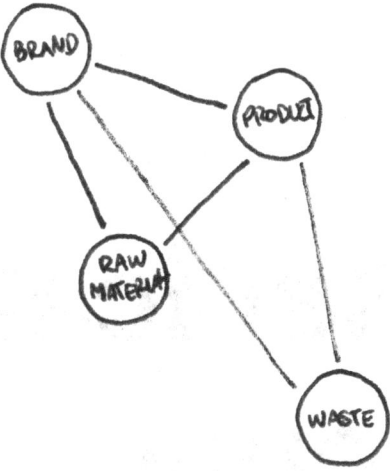

NOTES

19.   During the chaos of Lebanon's civil war, the country became a dumping ground for toxic waste. Foreign companies paid off Lebanese militia leaders for "permission" to dispose of many kinds of industrial chemicals from European nations (mainly Italy and Germany). Some of these dangerous wastes have been returned to the nations that produced them, but as Reese Erlich reports from Beirut, not all the imported toxins have been cleaned up. Living on Earth. "Lebanon: Toxic Waste Dumping Ground." Accessed May 2024, https://www.loe.org/shows/segments.html?programID=98-P13-00037&segmentID=2

20.   Téta is Arabic for "grandmother."

CHAPTER VII

Radical Gene- rosity

Cassette #7: Massive Attack

The album Protection *is playing on my Discman as I get myself ready to go to a protest against the Syrian occupation of Lebanon. The beats make my headphones pulsate and vibrate to the bass. It is the end of 2000, my last year in Lebanon before leaving for Paris. I draw my eyes with kohl and apply thick mascara to my lashes. My heart is in an endless wave of sadness as I savor the last moments of my life as I know it.*

In 1999, on the streets of Beirut, in front of the museum El Mathaf, walking distance from the new McDonald's, the youth were mobilizing. Around 20,000 young Lebanese were protesting the Syrian occupation. With our slogans we marched in unison; Lebanon would be free and independent from military occupation. We were walking side by side, women and girls in the center. It was an overwhelming moment. We were chanting with our posters held high, feeling the solidarity of all people who joined with us. Tears in our eyes, kohl slowly running down my cheeks, we were loudly demanding our sovereignty and our land back. As we continued to march, I documented the protest by taking photographs. A few people had camcorders and were recording the crowd.

Protesters started to alert the women and girls to move toward the center of the crowd as Syrian troops were seen approaching. Syrian tanks rolled through the streets of Beirut, targeting the crowd. Whispers guiding us toward safety and away from the protest allowed us to plan for a safe escape for the youngest there. Women and girls interlocked arms and began running in a diagonal to exit the larger group and retreat into alleyways. It was a radical act of generosity on the part of our elders to make a corridor for us to escape safely.

We hid behind a building and watched in horror as the Syrian military pummeled the protesters with water from high-pressure hoses. As the crowd dispersed, I heard gunshots in the distance. This was the climate I grew up in and that has remained a constant in protest. A very slow revolution that carried us throughout our lives. The military began roaming the streets looking for people to beat up and arrest while some of us found refuge in the nearby McDonald's. We ordered Turkish coffees and sundaes and started smoking. We discussed the fact that the Syrian Army was weaponizing our water, the result being that most of our population lived without readily available water for drinking or bathing.

After an afternoon that merged into a long night out strolling through Beirut, stopping in bars, and having long conversations on my friend's bed, I sneaked into my family apartment at three in the morning to an impeccably clean space. The aroma of incense and jasmine welcomed me home. I placed my keys gently on the hall table next to the altar. The living room's mosaic bowl filled with all the different packs of cigarettes available in the country was calling my name. I approached the bowl and marveled at our culture of care, even when it was offering cancerous delights. The bowl of cigarettes is sacred. It is purposefully curated to have every flavor of smoke available under the sun. Some are imported and bought from cigarette dealers on the streets, ensuring the host has all the options their guest might desire. In Lebanon, the radical act of generosity is a sacred act. The host takes care of their guests as if they were God in disguise. Sacred reciprocity has it so that every host in Lebanon follows this protocol and ritual; the cigarette bowl acts as a metaphor for the culture at large.

Sitting in the living room smoking, I thought about the protest, about my friends being harassed by the Syrian military, and about the ones who got arrested. We in Lebanon had been living in constant struggle for years, a struggle that forced us all to be on constant high alert. Coping through cigarettes was mandatory. Staring into the mosaic bowl, I was somewhere between meditation and dissociation. What was one more cigarette? One for the memories we would probably forget, trapped behind the mountain of shame the next explosion would create.

I lit my Marlboro Light on the balcony, having made my way there tiptoeing over the pristine marble floors reflecting my being like mirrors, holding my breath until I reached the white plastic chairs and the small low tables outside. There I smoked and looked at the night sky filled with stars; the electricity had just gone out and Beirut was now submerged in total darkness. I could see the cosmos from there. My heart was in shambles. I knew I would soon be leaving this magical and complicated country. Overwhelmed with the certitude that all I knew would be seen as nothing more than folklore at best and that I would have to wear multiple layers of armor to survive the West and be seen as an equal. No matter how many languages I spoke, or how well I could adapt and immerse myself in the West, I knew I would never truly belong.

I stubbed out my cigarette and brought the butt inside to carefully dispose of it. We didn't flick cigarette butts off the balcony. When the neighbors' roosters sang their morning song, my grandmother's friends would begin cleaning their balconies, watering their plants, and feeding their urban chickens. If they were to find a cigarette on their pristine veranda, they would be able to trace it back to the person who threw it. And I certainly wouldn't want to be that person. We are brought up to show consideration for our community. Our mothers teach us women to care for others. Men and boys have their own responsibilities; they are raised to be helpful and strong in ways women aren't expected to be. But women are raised to hold their community spiritually and physically. Keeping an impeccably clean home is one of these responsibilities, and preparing our ancestral food is another.

The lessons I was taught while growing up in Lebanon were centered on radical generosity and radical reciprocity. These same principles aren't taught the same way (or at all) in cultures of the Global North. The extractive nature of the overarching belief system in the West is often justified by tales and paradigms supporting an extractive and linear relationship with the earth and a hyperindividualistic notion of the self as separate from nature and only made valuable by amassed possessions.

In my culture, sharing resources is the norm, being a community-centered system. After the war, we shared food, internet access, and cable TV access. Electricity cuts happened regularly due to continued bombing of our electric facilities by the Israeli military. The constant bombing created a broken infrastructure that over time has become more and more vulnerable to attack and harder to repair. The repairs are exponentially more expensive each time they are required, which has resulted in an ongoing lack of electricity. This means that community-led solutions such as sharing generators (or *moteur* as they are called in French but pronounced with a heavy Lebanese accent rolling the r's) are absolutely necessary. Each neighborhood has designated families who have taken the responsibility of fronting the cost of a generator to provide electricity locally to their neighbors, collectively then sharing cost and energy.

A similar situation in the Global North would be handled differently. Folks would be forced to act individually, making it too expensive for each household to own generators. This would potentially result in lack of resources for some and a level of extreme injustice that does not exist in Lebanon. The individualistic solutions employed in the Global North not only consume more energy but are excessive, expensive, and unnecessary. Collective systems based on the sharing economy are often discouraged and rendered illegal. Community coalitions and resilient programs rooted in the simple concept of taking care of one another at the expense of profit are often criminalized in places like France, Canada, and the United States. These are places where an individualistic consumer-driven culture that forbids the act of sharing is favored.

In Lebanon you can negotiate prices and even barter with the generator man to provide equitably to all the neighbors needing electricity when the government fails to provide for its citizens. People fill in the blank of a failed government. Corporations and startups are rendered obsolete when communities find themselves needing to adapt to ongoing disasters. Human-to-human solutions based on a case-by-case understanding negotiated individually or sometimes collectively in order to ensure an equitable share of resources are the framework that the North dreads the most. We work with case-by-case frameworks of radical generosity and reciprocity that rend the fabric of colonial oppression. Distributed systems of care are very effective at disempowering controlling and exploitative systems.

Since the great exodus of the 1980s, our roles have expanded beyond being responsible for basic necessities. As of this moment in 2023, 75 percent of Lebanese people live outside their country. There has been a massive brain drain, which has left mainly the elderly still living in our ancestral land. Everyone who plans on leaving experiences angst. Both staying and leaving require an immense amount of responsibility to give back and hold our people. During the war, my grandfather's shelter became a safe haven for our nearby neighbors. Everyone who came brought offerings to share, sometimes risking their own lives to secure the basic necessities as militias rationed bread and water at various checkpoints. To negotiate bigger allowances, one had to be gifted with the wit and negotiation skills necessary for survival, like being able to read the room and knowing what to say and when to say it. Everything is negotiable in the Global South, especially in Lebanon, where governments act as military decorations imposing outdated ideologies held by dying warlords hanging on until the end.

My earliest memories are in that shelter. I don't know if I actually remember, or if I imagine I remember when my grandfather reminds me: I was three years old, dancing to entertain the neighbors. We were eating Picon cheese rolled in Lebanese pita bread. The cigarette smoke served as a veil, obscuring the worried faces of the adults like characters in a Renaissance painting hiding in the shadows cast by candlelight. The cold, damp air in the shelter contrasted with the warm hugs of my grandmother. Women held their communities with their energy, locking eyes with everyone in a gesture that offered refuge and comfort. They made sure we were all okay even if nobody was truly okay. Compassionate eye contact would hold us for a while. As we sat and waited for the bombing to cease, an "Allah karim" echoed in the space—"God is generous"—one of my father's sayings borrowed from his mother (my grandmother Souad). We never allowed ourselves to despair. God was generous, and so was Nature.

God and Nature and Us—the original holy trinity, perhaps.

In ancient times, long before the Romans occupied our lands, Nature was God, and the many gods were Nature. Later through the Abrahamic religions, the many gods became one God, a son of another God. All stemming from the same source, a generous source that gives infinitely. Our culture worships this inherent understanding of generosity. We are constantly receiving, as God is generous, so how are we reciprocating? That is the essence of our savoir vivre. How can we give back? To each other and to Nature?

As Lebanese people, we compete with each other to be the most generous. For instance, after a meal at a restaurant, after long hours spent dancing and singing to "Reja3 Reja3 yet3amar Lebnan"—the call for hope that establishes a hopeful future for Lebanon—a fight will break out for the *fettoura*, the check. People will actually fight to pay for their friends. Pushing each other and screaming with a genuine desire to cover the bill and honor the other person. Because God is generous, indeed, and so are we.

The same situation in the Global North is often filled with awkwardness, a concept I believe only exists in Anglo-Saxon cultures. To feel awkward is to know decorum and politeness as a form of repression, which upholds a lack of generosity. In my personal experience in the Global North, I would pay for my friends at lunch or dinner, only to realize that they gladly took advantage of me since they had no intention whatsoever of reciprocating this gesture, ever. My loss, so to speak. I learned the hard way that to sustain friendships with people living in France, the United Kingdom, Canada, and the United States, I had to hold back on generosity. That felt like removing an entire part of myself. However, remaining whole would lead me to disappointing situations where the other party righteously took advantage of my kindness. If I felt taken advantage of, it would be my own doing. Did I set them up to fail by being too generous? Living in a world where giving was a transaction felt like shrinking. Because I'd lived with the expansive belief that God is generous, as is my community, being confronted with the opposite belief felt like a slow death.

The Giving Tree by Shel Silverstein is a great example of the individualistic approach the Global North has toward taking from nature, and by extension each other, without reciprocating. It is a core belief of Western ideology that positions the white man above all forms of life on earth, all creatures, and all living things. The pain and angst Silverstein's main character feels is depicted as his insatiable desire to receive, and his belief that all life is centered around his personal comfort and well-being. He does not once consider giving back, which results in the tragedy of his loneliness and death. By the end of the book he has learned nothing and destroyed everything. Some argue that The Giving Tree is written as a critique of this way of life, while others see it as an artifact normalizing violent individualism and Eurocentric extractionist values. It is clear to me that generosity without a clear understanding of reciprocity invites the colonized mind to pillage—to benefit from generosity without participating. Our relationship with nature depends on our culture and the stories we tell our children and ourselves.

Although I have followed an untraditional career path through many twists and turns, I consider myself first an artist. And a fundamental role of the artist is to ask the broadest, most important questions. Some of the questions that have driven my work over the past two decades are: (1) Can we bring people closer to the current overlapping issues that create the fabric of our collective existential crises? (2) Can we agree that climate change will create a series of climate disasters, and do we have enough time to enact the necessary changes needed? (3) Can the data collected become more personal? (4) Can we communicate the urgency in a poetic and inspiring way? (5) Can science become understood by all?

I have been asking myself these questions most of my life: As a teenager protesting the Syrian regime. As a young adult making her path in life. As a young mother in her twenties seeing the grimmest predictions of climate change and pollution from my childhood begin to manifest on a global scale. As an artist wondering what the roles for our collective liberation might be, and if art could be a pathway toward systemic change. I was interested in creating a generous body of work that would allow for the necessary seeds, frameworks, and blueprints to be used as a fertile offering to the current and next generations. I was also hoping that perhaps my work would be fruitful enough to be a catalyst and to disrupt, reroute, dismantle, and reorganize current systems responsible for the climate and political crises we are all being subjected to. It seemed to me that the very system itself was designed at the opposite end of generosity.

Experiencing the world on the fringes of collapsing colonial empires has afforded many of us who have lived through it a sharpness of perception that translates into the ability to provide much-needed perspective. We have embraced the intense aspects of our survival and the many skills generously given to us that make up the fabric of our being. This is what gives us the ability to make a contribution to this planet. I am speaking here of the Global Majority of people whose existence is purposefully erased, oppressed, and marginalized for the benefit of the few powers at the very top of this disturbing global pyramid scheme. Many conversations have led me to becoming more emboldened in my perception of these injustices and in being able to speak out, and most importantly, radically imagine the roads ahead.

The role of the artist is key in creating new worlds because we have the ability to see what's ahead and to make sense of it all. Although my parents had strongly discouraged me from pursuing a path as an artist, I couldn't help it from manifesting in me. Even though I was told that I was "too conceptual" for the applied arts school I was attending, and that I was not a practical designer they could train to be a straightforward functioning member of society, I couldn't allow myself to go to a conceptual school focused solely on fine arts; this wasn't something that was "for me," as my parents put it.

"Art, you see, is not for us," they said. "We need to be useful and functional in society. You must find a way to put the many skills God has given you into a productive path."

I had cried myself a river as I discussed what my options might be with my mentor Patrick André depuis 1966. I returned to my apartment to find my father, the tallest and strongest man I knew, crouched on a small chair, his knees practically touching the ceiling of my miniscule studio apartment. His stare was decisive. He was coming to pull me out of this dream.

"You have two choices," he said. "You can either go to Montreal and study in a university and work your way into a career, or you can come back with me to Beirut and study there to become a teacher."

I was devastated by my options only because my calling was to be an artist. None of them seemed to lead me there. I chose to go to Montreal since I couldn't bear the thought of going to Beirut to become a teacher. This path seemed like total death. While in Montreal I bounced from one university to another and finally created my own open-ended bachelor's degree in communications and cyberarts, which was a sort of new media/applied arts discipline allowing me to focus on concrete projects while maintaining an artistic approach. It was like art was flowing in every direction. I felt so close to my calling by just allowing art to be my life. This was not quite as rewarding as being an "artist;" nonetheless, I was able to create, and that brought me joy.

When I got the fateful phone call from my mother telling me the Israeli army had bombed the Lebanese airport in the summer of 2006, I understood what my parents meant when they said art was not for us. I understood the feeling that the insecurity of a purely creative career seemed like a luxury we didn't have, that we had to find ways to survive and sustain ourselves through resiliency. This meant being able to provide for ourselves and others, to be a shelter for others. Lebanese people were fleeing once again, seeking refuge on boats leaving the port of Beirut heading toward Cyprus and other countries. My parents decided to stay; they were the refuge for their parents and siblings.

The summer when my sister and I were stranded in Montreal away from our family in Beirut was like a slap in the face, and it slapped the art out of me. I needed to be serious, to be reliable, and to be able to hold my family and be their shelter. I couldn't do any of that while being a vulnerable artist working many jobs and creating works only a few could relate to or afford. I put my portfolio aside; I hid my digital work on an external hard drive and wiped my computer clean.

But my journey away from a career in Art, perhaps infused my life with art instead. The art of design communication, the art of interface design, the art of information architecture; as these fields grew and developed in the evolving connected world, I also evolved as a designer and as a person.

The web and the internet culture I had been a part of since the beginning of the 2000s was all about open access, open knowledge, and the radical openness of all boundaries, from digital to physical to international. Man-made boundaries had no power over the internet; they had to be hard coded and imposed, or ignored and left to rot in the physical world.

It was an exciting time for prototyping, launching new radical ideas, and growing global movements. I never felt more at home than when I was online. The internet community I was in, both digital and physical, made me feel like I finally belonged. All the idealist geeks who knew how to create things and make them happen, and espoused concepts of radical generosity made me feel safe for the first time in the West. I devoted my entire twenties to creating pathways to digital access and literacy for communities in the Middle East and North Africa and particularly on the ground in Lebanon. Giving our youth internet access and digital cameras, teaching them how to code and to use digital software to design, gave my life so much more purpose. I was able to translate and bridge East and West, empower people by giving them access to tools that could change the course of their lives and careers, but also inspire them to use these tools for collective liberation. My work in digital literacy was all about giving information and opening new roads. The ethics of radical openness and of distributed networks were grounded in the principles of radical generosity and reciprocity.

The Principles of Open Knowledge

1. *Sharing knowledge.* Gatekeepers are obsolete. Sharing knowledge is a human right.

2. *Giving back.* If you benefit or learn from the knowledge of a group, you must contribute back to it—adding value to the collective.

3. *Linking back to sources.* Citing your sources has been a staple of academia for millennia, but in a digital context it means to point back via hyperlink to the original source of a given concept or piece of information or code. Everything is a remix, but there are clear sources that instigate new paths. Mention them.

4. *Leaving clear traces.* Similar to the previous point of linking back, do not erase codes, URLs, and information, and do not create holes in the fabric of information. Leave breadcrumbs to connect the dots.

These principles rely on compassion and community-driven concepts of democracy and radical generosity. Knowing your limit and source of energy is key to spreading out into generosity, and knowing your boundaries enough to understand what nourishment or self-nourishment you need enables generosity that strengthens you rather than depletes you. If the fabric of the web were broken by any or all violations of the abovementioned principles, the strength of the collective knowledge would become weaker and would not uphold the progress and innovation needed to sustain the internet. The way technology and innovation grew exponentially during that period depended on these principles and the fact that collective knowledge and equity is far more robust than privatized solutions that benefit only a few. Radical generosity without radical reciprocity is an exploitation and abuse of kindness. In the context of the internet, that would mean breaking the web of knowledge that holds and generates all the connections necessary for the internet to prosper.

I was passionate about this community and constantly contributing to the commons, sharing knowledge, linking back to others, and building a tight network of peers and friends. We hired each other, brainstormed ideas, and sometimes fell in love with one another. Around that time (2007), as I was working in my second agency on digital literacy, Massive Attack playing in the loft space, my boss and I fell in love. It was like the encounter of two species from different galaxies meeting and, against all odds, falling in love.

When I met Colin, they had been polyamorous and bi-sexual for over a decade, living communally with others in relationships that adhered to the tenants of total and radical generosity. They embodied radical giving and experienced polyamory as the expression of ultimate expansion and freedom. Sadly, I wasn't able to embrace it. I couldn't bear the thought of sharing my partner with anyone else. I observed polyamory from a distance, both fascinated and curious, yet unable to participate. And for many months our love was only platonic and grounded in mutual respect and admiration.

The company I was working with was owned by Colin and his partner (both brilliant musicians), who built their company—one of the most successful agencies in Montreal at the time—from the ground up. Colin, like many engineers, had learned to code and built complex systems from peer-to-peer learning and hacking. I was designing, and Colin and his teams were coding. The closer the collaboration between design and engineer, the better the system would be. Seamless and straight-forward. And so, we built many systems together, merging our skills and our cultures within each project. Every project we created had the mission to share knowledge, information, and access to distributed governance and empower different communities to create their own work.

Before we fell in love, we were friends and had no intention of jeopardizing our work relationship or friend-ship. And even when we became aware that we were falling madly in love with one another, we kept it platonic for nine months straight.

During this time, in 2008, while brainstorming a new project with Colin, I came up with the concept for Slow Factory. It was a response to the rise of the fast companies and fast everything that followed the launch of the first iPhones. Everything was becoming faster than ever—and so Slow Factory was born with the intention to "slow down and look at the big picture." I asked if Colin could reserve the domain name for me, which he did, and our first art project together was born. From 2008 until the official launch of Slow Factory on August 8, 2012, the website had a full-screen video playing on a loop that Colin shot of a boat very, very slowly traversing the Fleuve Saint-Laurent in Montreal at night. So slowly, in fact, its movements were barely perceptible.

Initially the romance between me and Colin didn't work out—I couldn't open up to polyamory and Colin couldn't become exclusive to me—so I ran away to New York where I started a new job at a digital agency. It was a corporate job designing large sites for major global brands and retailers, and I learned a lot. I got to build large systems and work on information architecture and strategy. All the skills and experience I gained there, I used to fully bring Slow Factory into being many years later. As I walked to the bus stop in Brooklyn to get to my work, I would look at my shadow on the pavement, following me around, and feel it was Colin's spirit tied to me somehow.

At the end of 2008 I flew to Lebanon for the holidays. Of course, it was a secret to my mother that Colin and I had had a relationship that resulted in a miscarriage, an awful breakup, and my running away to New York.

However, I apparently talked about him enough to pique my mother's interest, and at a coffee ceremony one morning, she asked, "What is it that makes this Colin person so memorable?"

The only answer that came to me was "His generosity. He is generous like us."

When I returned to New York, I walked across the street from my apartment to visit my dear friend Gina, who was a Roma fortune teller. My radical generosity resulted in me giving her my entire salary for the month of December while I lived on credit so she could buy presents for her children. Through the course of our friendship, I taught her and her children how to read and write. The Roma people, a persecuted nomadic tribe from Eastern Europe, had for centuries been ethnically cleansed to the point where they had been uprooted and were now dispersed around the world. New York had a large diaspora of Roma folks who traditionally carried wisdom and knowledge from mother to daughter, particularly on clairvoyance and spiritual knowledge.

Gina smoked and looked at me in that way she had that made me feel like she could read my spirit. Her long, straight blond hair floated around her face, and her eyebrows, which were drawn to perfection, twitched slightly. She said, "Colin is not done with you, he's looking for you. And he's coming here to New York City."

I was stunned. We weren't in touch. We didn't have each other's new phone numbers and I changed my email address when I arrived in Brooklyn. "Impossible," I responded. "He doesn't know where I am."

Gina looked amused, and said, "Did I ever tell you anything that didn't happen? I know he's looking for you because his spirit is tied to yours. He will find you before January comes."

I left her feeling confused and scared and went for a walk to clear my head. *Impossible. Impossible. There is no way he can find me.* When I returned home, I remembered a Flickr account Colin had made for me. It turned out that Colin had dedicated a photo a day to me on this secret account since I'd left Montreal. There was one for my birthday, many for random things he did that I knew made him think of me because he was posed in places we went together. There were photos of vinyls we listened to and books we read. The most recent post was a photo of Colin with hands splayed out showing off their black nail polish.

I commented with a photo of myself making the same gesture. Realizing immediately how stupid that was, I erased it right away.

A new comment appeared. "It's Colin," it said. "I saw you."

Somewhere on the internet, on slowfactory.com, a very low boat was crossing the screen from one side to another, peacefully and silently traversing the river at night.

I never intended to share my love story with Colin publicly. Our wedding was very discreet and intimate. Once we got together, our world changed. Colin and his business partner parted ways after 7 years. I lost some of my core friendships, formative friends who had been present throughout my twenties. Colin and I found ourselves alone together, with rocky relationships with both of our families. We only had our shared vision of life holding us together.

I learned English later in my life, and with Colin spoke both French and English. But I knew that if Colin truly wanted to understand my culture, he would need to learn Arabic to embrace my world. To my surprise, Colin was already learning how to read Arabic on his own, treating the language like a new code.

In the months that followed the birth of our first child, Sila Grey, we went to Lebanon and stayed for close to a year. Building a relationship with my elders and living in Lebanon for a few years, on and off, as we figured things out was how we approached radical generosity and the notion of reciprocity and respect. Colin was attending Arabic school, driving around Beirut, and Sila and I were spending time with my elders and collecting stories, some that have ended up in this book.

In February 2012, a month after Sila was born, I began connecting the dots in a tiny notebook I was carrying around. A lot of the pages detailed vivid dreams clearly identifying the field I was going to be working in: Fashion, which made no sense. "Open source" and "open knowledge for fashion" kept coming back in my dreams. I was trying to make sense of the many areas of interest I had and the skills I'd amassed so far in the course of my eclectic career.

A deep sense of belonging was often missing in my life, which made me run in survival mode. I was uprooted at such a young age, and the feeling of being disconnected never truly left my body. But now that I was in Beirut, I was finally feeling grounded enough to look back at my past to better understand my future. Looking back at the past for this purpose is common Indigenous practice, and for people whose indigeneity is questioned or lost—like most of us in our region who survived thousands of years of ongoing occupation, cultural cleansing, and oppression—remembering our traditional knowledge helps us ground ourselves and reorient us toward our future. I was connecting the dots between open-source knowledge and fashion, waste, environmentalism, social justice, design, and art. A constellation of seemingly unrelated topics began to emerge on paper. Its formation, like a nebula, began to make sense to me. In the process of creating meaning for Slow Factory, the new entity that started to form past that slow-motion video of a boat, a structure of idea, an offering became clear. Slow Factory would generously offer meaning and connection between people and their environment.

Nine years later, a few months before the eighth anniversary of Slow Factory in August 2020, the world was on lockdown due to the COVID-19 pandemic. On the 4th of

August, at the Port of Beirut, a fire erupted in a storage unit where ammonium nitrate was being illegally stored. The fire sparked an explosion that was estimated to be as strong as a 3.3 magnitude earthquake. The damage from the blast affected more than half of Beirut, displacing 300,000 people and killing thousands. It was one of the largest nonnuclear explosions ever recorded.

I found out about the explosion by scrolling through Instagram and seeing a video of it on a loop on a friend's account. I froze and couldn't make sense of it. At that same moment, a WhatsApp text message appeared on my screen. It was my sister informing me that her home in Beirut had "exploded." My heart sank deep in my body. I was unable to move or speak; all I could do was pass the phone to Colin. The pain we felt was irrelevant, to be honest, next to the real pain our family was going through on the ground. Not being able to be there, not being useful, not being able to clean the streets and repair homes with our friends was infuriating. How many times had I been stuck in the Global North while my heart and soul were in Lebanon?

I wasn't able to eat or sleep while I mobilized from New York to help our community in Beirut. I fundraised, wrote articles, posted relevant information, but no matter how much I did, it wasn't enough, and I knew it. My mother and a few of her friends spent time cooking hundreds of meals a day, offering them at no cost to anyone who needed them. Every morning they would prepare and package hundreds of containers containing delicious, fresh Lebanese food. This wasn't about my mom making delicious meals; this was her working for God. Everyone was giving beyond their capabilities, and Lebanese expats, refugees, and immigrants abroad all mobilized to send money and resources and provide support to build renewable energy projects to sustain folks as the electricity cuts post-explosion were unbearable in the heat of the summer, rendering most of the food inedible.

The Lebanese government was nowhere to be found. The streets after the explosion were covered with a white dust, the air was thick, every single glass window was broken, doors and windows were concave and in need of professional repair. The streets were cleaned by the neighborhood children and young folks, while Lebanese government officials hid in their mansions.

The radical generosity of the people and their vigilant support of one another became the backbone of our collective well-being. Folks in Lebanon and outside the country worked in tandem to support the necessary rebuilding efforts of homes before the rainy season that often starts mid-September. Communal spaces where solar panels were being installed provided electricity for a dozen communal fridges and phone chargers. Safe spaces to rest, couches, and bathrooms were made available to workers providing on-the-ground support.

These radical acts of generosity were inherently nontransactional. If they had been, they wouldn't be qualified as acts of generosity. People were keen on giving and on providing for others in ways that were grounded in trust. A deep sense of trust that their deeds were being appreciated and accounted for in a bigger way. The generous model we in Lebanon seem to be relying on, one that doesn't exist in the West and in the Global North, really stems from an understanding that God is generous. No matter how we interact with scarcity, we know it is temporary, for the generosity of this planet is inherent in its nature and requires that we change the paradigm that has brought us to believe otherwise.

CHAPTER VIII

Un-
learning
War

Cassette #8: Grandfather Labib

His voice is recorded on a cassette tape plastered with a white sticker stuck over a pile of white stickers, with a message written in Arabic "For Ghada," my mother. This is the same tape we had sent to Beirut and that is returning to us in Montreal brought by a Lebanese traveler coming from Beirut. This was how we communicated with family back home. Phone lines in Beirut were constantly bombed, and this was long before the internet existed. The tape begins with a message recorded over the message we had recorded. It begins with: "Beirut is divided, chaos in every way ... but don't worry about us, we are together, and we are keeping each other safe. We loved hearing the kids sing on the previous message. My God, we love them so much. Keep sending us their voices. We miss you."

As I am writing these words, at the end of 2023, genocide is occurring in Gaza and war looms over Lebanon. Living in a perpetual climate of uncertainty has imprinted my worldview, my life, and the decisions I have made in both my career and personal life. We grew up being wary of whatever consensus the mainstream media adopted and how we were portrayed. From a very young age I understood the value of being surrounded by a trustworthy community, especially in the midst of tragedy. I also learned to gain as much perspective and context as possible in order to comprehend a given situation. I favored a mosaic of perspectives and stories and embraced plurality and nuances, which is what was constantly omitted from stories told by mainstream media.

My earliest memories as well as most of my life's defining moments have been punctuated by war. Wars, or what Western media likes to call "conflicts" or "crises in the Middle East," are designed to decimate my people, "wipe them off the face of the earth," as Israeli Prime Minister Netanyahu has repeated on television multiple times. War has been a constant in my life—a form of certitude—

like rain; war will come, and it will change everything. Every single war has annihilated every aspect of normalcy and projected us (me, my family, my people) into a perpetual state of panic and survival. So much so that panic and survival have become the default state of my bruised nervous system, which carries the imprints of war and damage in its core.

Every time bombs began raining down on me and my family, if we were safe enough to gather around the television powered by the generator, "Mr. Moteur," next door, we tuned into the Lebanese channels, where anchors generally reported the news their network had approved. The religious denomination of TV networks as well as their political orientation would sway information left, right, and center depending on their own agenda. Journalism has always been subjective, despite what the Global North would like to force feed us to believe. There isn't any objectivity in war, and politics cannot function in a vacuum. Watching the news meant watching multiple channels simultaneously while piecing together the truth from various points of view and narratives. That was the closest we could get to "objectivity"—embracing plurality and the notion of perspectives and subjectivity.

Watching the news was a great activity: with such intermittent access to electricity, gathering around the television was essential. Debating, sharing stories, and contradicting the news anchors was a test of our rhetorical ability and fluency in geopolitics. It was important to witness the fabricated storytelling that was labeling our people as "terrorists," a term used to justify those who would murder our people with impunity. Family members and neighbors would become voice-over commentators denouncing false narratives. This often resulted in everybody yelling at the screen and then eventually at each other. We passionately argued for our points of view and theories of change. The fact that my community could contradict the news anchors with firsthand information that was never shown on television helped me understand that the media wasn't an objective authority, people were. If my community disagreed with the anchor on television, it meant that the truth was being manipulated.

This opened my mind to the possibility of changing people's perspectives and the necessity of fostering a global community that was empowered to share their messages and truths. Citizen journalism wasn't a combination of words I knew until my twenties when this concept became a core part of my reality, especially in the wake of the Arab Spring when we collectively took back our stories.

Before the internet existed, we had access to multiple sources of information on television by way of a pirated satellite dish, which allowed my community to become the local commentators they needed. They wove stories and facts together in a way that gave a more truthful and sophisticated perspective on our history. For instance, during the decades of the Lebanese Civil war, "They are all the same! Each side sounds the same!" would often be shouted at the television, highlighting the turbulent state we were in, where kin were set to murder one another and where instability and violence constituted the fabric of our reality. This was the ultimate expression of the divide-and-conquer framework of oppression largely adopted by the subjugated peoples of the former European colonies. It was a form of internalized colonialism that served the Global North. By hating on ourselves to pass as "modern," we weaponized our differences and murdered one another.

War is not the greatest equalizer; it accentuates the differences that already exist. For instance, there are people who lose their entire families, and then there are people who are surrounded and protected by their own personal militia. There are people who become houseless, and ones who own the entire block; those who have to flee by boat, risking their lives and often drowning in the Mediterranean Sea, and ones with foreign passports who can leave by plane with a first-class ticket. Stories we tell ourselves or that others tell about us tend to shape our reality and our circumstances. American and mainstream European media make sense of the war by dehumanizing our people to justify atrocities inflicted upon us, centering their own safety and comfort at our expense. We witness this time and time again.

I was born in a war that shook me from the womb of my mother, and that altered the lives of my parents who lived in terror and constant anticipation of another apocalypse. The war attempted to erase their dreams, and the dreams of their families and community, crushing them under the weight of pain and suffering. War has attempted to silence us for decades, trapping us in a time capsule of pain, dust, blood, decay, and smoke. We were wrapped in the garbage of nearby countries who disposed of their filth on our land with total impunity, a practice commonly known as waste colonialism. European countries took part in this dese- cration while our people starved. Instead of receiving food, we received their garbage.

The erasure and dehumanization of Arab people and culture serves a fabricated "peace" at the expense of mil- lions of people. Palestinians suffer under an inhumane siege, subjected to what is really ethnic cleansing; Syrians suffer a never-ending war; and Lebanese live without wa- ter or electricity in a broken country waiting to be bombed as part of the Israeli collective punishment strategy, an extension of the US war machine. The last time Arabs were compared to animals on television, the Iraqis paid the price in 2001 for 9/11. Over a million human beings were slaughtered by the US military.

I witnessed the Iraq war on the new television my father gave me as a housewarming present when I relo- cated to Montreal after my infamous year in Paris. I re- corded the broadcast as a way to dissect it once again and to allow my family to comment on it while recording our sporadic conversations over the phone. I felt completely helpless as I watched the American military's state-of- the-art artillery murder, from a safe distance, hundreds of thousands of Iraqis—men, women and children alike— as if they were playing a video game. CNN and other channels would broadcast Americans and foreigners safely stealing Iraqi cultural treasures, looting archaeological sites and illegally—at least according to the Geneva Accords—pillaging UNESCO World Heritage sites.

My heart sank as I watched the atrocities being committed. I missed my community of commentators, my citizen journalists. I needed them to give me their perspective on the situation. Sobbing and watching alone, I felt a deep sense of betrayal. During that time, I was attending multiple universities at once, gathering as much perspective as I could, and thus reluctantly shutting the television off while leaving a VHS tape in to record the news while I was away from home. The feeling of being alienated and othered was both familiar and a condition I was working to shake off. The contradictions in our realities present a constant and a comfort for me—certitude can be synonymous with fascism and violence. Why can't I relate with anyone?

Most of my classmates were oblivious to the Iraq war. They were living in comfort and ease and were able to calmly focus on their classes. Fascinating to me, who lived with a war inside. I've always suffered from chronic agitation, perhaps undiagnosed ADHD. I recall some of my primary school teachers warning my mother that I was unable to sit down, that I was hyperactive and couldn't focus. Teachers often seemed to be ganging up on me and trying to eradicate me by transferring me to the "undesirable kids' classroom" for some reason. I tried so hard to catch up, to quickly learn the new language. I've never been able to quiet the tornado inside me.

It was true, I could barely sit still. And thus, even in my early twenties, during the war in Iraq, my mind was spinning while I was trying to focus on lectures given in large dark auditoriums filled with people who couldn't care less about what is happening in the world, let alone that an unjust war, a military occupation and theft of historical artifacts, a genocide, was happening in the Middle East. During our breaks I would engage with my classmates outside while everyone smoked cigarettes. I asked if anyone was aware that a war was raging and received only nonchalant looks. These looks were then sometimes followed by an interrogation to see if I were on the side of the terrorists that caused 9/11.

"It's a war against terrorism," someone would say. "You want the terrorists to come here?" someone else would ask.

I had no words to respond to these abject incongruities and racist remarks. I would absorb all that was said and marinate in it.

When people ask us if we support terrorism when discussing illegal and unjustified military invasions in our lands, we know too well the racism behind these interrogations. The colonial playbook knows who to dehumanize and how to create a hierarchy of oppression designed to silence anyone who dares to speak out against injustices. Arabs will be sacrificed for the oil machine that pollutes and destroys our planet. While we pray for those who have lost their lives at the hands of violence and apartheid, we know the only way out is by radically imagining new systems that center our humanity and nature, and by radically building them in a regenerative way. Until then we breathe and pray.

Colonial Military Occupiers have compared us to animals in order to subject us to the same fate the sacred bison on Turtle Island were subjected to at the hands of the European colonizers. In 1871 one colonel told a wealthy hunter who felt a shiver of guilt after he shot thirty bulls in one trip: "Kill every buffalo you can! Every buffalo dead is an Indian gone." Native peoples relied on the bison for everything from food and clothing, to shelter and religious worship. They used almost every part of the animal, including horns, meat, and tail hairs. The desecration of all creation allows for colonial dominance over Indigenous peoples and the animal world, whether in the Americas or in the Middle East.

Buffalo Bill Cody, who was hired to kill the sacred animals, slaughtered more than 4,000 bison in less than two years. To defeat Native Americans and steal their land, US government officials actively destroyed bison and encouraged settlers to hunt and kill them en masse, which decimated them and brought them to the brink of extinction. US Army officers ordered troops to kill bison as a means to deprive Native Americans a vital source of food. Oral histories of the tragedy consist of haunting recollections of the horror settlers inflicted on the Native population and the bison. These stories were left out of history books and formal colonial education. At first, colonizers denied it ever happened.

The colonial paradigm that justifies ongoing wars is based on a misunderstanding of biblical myths: The origin stories settlers tell themselves are that man was created in the image of a righteous god, a violent god and a god that although loving could be a vengeful god demanding the total subjugation of man. That god told them to go conquer the lands and smite their enemies. From the rib of that man, the colonial god created the settler woman. She would uphold the will of their god and would hold the burden of life and creation through shame, blame, and suffering. The origin story elaborates on the misunderstanding that God then gave man the animal and plant kingdoms and the natural world to dominate, while purposefully separating man from the animal kingdom. The original separation of nature and man, man and woman, and God above all, constitutes the ultimate pyramid scheme that allows for colonial dominance of people and planet. White men at the top of the pyramid and all life forms at the bottom, neatly organized into categories, their oppression hierarchized, and their value limited to criteria predetermined by the very group of elite white men at the top.

Our collective liberation from this paradigm of violent hierarchization, segregation, and utter misunderstanding of life and creation resides in our ability to radically unlearn it—thus unlearning the doctrine of domination itself. In the same spirit, the so-called animal kingdom doesn't deserve to be subjugated to the settler man and decimated to extinction. We are all sacred. The balance is not going to come from gaining approval and elevating our status to the white man; it's about upholding the sacredness of our lives in connection with each other and with the world and nature that surrounds us, completely outside the colonial paradigm. In fact, the proposition for collective liberation is to transform the triangle of oppression into a circle, a spiral, of liberation and interconnectedness.

This version of Abrahamic God is often portrayed as the Father, the patriarch; and where the Western cultures have taken this to build an oppressive Partriarchy, I see as a misunderstanding of the Divine Masculine, holding and supporting the collective with a generous strength, a strength that I have felt from my father.

I have only ever felt safe in the arms of my father. My gorgeous father whose teenage years were abruptly interrupted by the war in Lebanon. At eighteen, his mandatory military service was cut short, his cohort advised to take whatever weapons and equipment they could get their hands on and run back to their neighborhoods to protect their families. Shortly after arriving at his family home, he found out that his uncle had been kidnapped. Later, his dead body was discovered and it was obvious that he had been subjected to torture. His uncle's crime was his religion. The war had turned brothers against one another. One's religion could be enough of an incentive to murder, rape, and erase the entire bloodline related to that person. My father's life has also been punctuated by wars and by the act of fleeing to find safety. A constant refugee, always living in temporary housing from his teenage years all the way into his seventies. When your home seems to turn against you, that is an ongoing betrayal that remains ingrained within you. When I close my eyes and look for shelter, I see an image of my father carrying all three of us on his shoulders and in his arms—my sister, myself, and my little brother—carrying us to safety.

As I write this book, another war is raging in Palestine and is spilling over into Lebanon. I know my father is spiritually holding my sister's three children on his back and in his arms, carrying them to safety far from the bombardment. He is holding my sister's and mother's hands in each of his. To me, Arab men like my father are the archetype of the Divine Masculine. A man who cried in front of us while watching the news and when he was given a pair of sneakers for Christmas after he'd braved death during open-heart surgery. He has risen from the rubble time and time again, the rubble of our destroyed home, the rubble of his career paths.

His handsome face is imprinted on mine, we have the same eyes, nose, and hair. Men in our culture are soft inside. They carry both the Divine Masculine and the Divine Feminine. I have been so lucky to witness true masculine energy in my father and the men of my culture. The stereotypes fabricated about us in the West are wrong. Our men nurture us, hold us, and carry us as children. And when we become adults, they are the first to hold space for us, even as our mothers may object. Fathers open new roads for their daughters and allow us to go beyond our collective imagination. They teach us about money, about drinking, and confide in us as if they were recording their stories on a human tape recorder. I hold their stories. I hear their stories while sharing space in total silence, we can hear their thoughts, and they allow us to hear them.

During times of war, money becomes practically obsolete; people turn to each other to provide and share resources: bread, water, electricity, fuel, shelter. Money, designed to uphold individualism, tends to encourage a separation between the ones who are fortunate and the ones who aren't. In times of war, however, this separation becomes a matter of life or death. And as much as we witness indescribable horrors, there are divine masculine and divine feminine energies at play protecting, holding, healing, nurturing, and saving one another. Money can also be used to flee danger, to buy a way out of the chaos. For this reason my father left my mother in Beirut to go work in Saudi Arabia to make enough money to get her out of Lebanon. It was a long-distance relationship, with one living under the bombs and the other in the desert.

Later, my mother joined him in Jeddah, Saudi Arabia. Two young people who fell in love at first sight—three months later married during a short ceasefire. On December 25, 1981, they had a Christmas wedding following a humanitarian pause to allow for aid to enter the country. There is an iconic picture of my father carrying my mother, who wore a simple yet gorgeous white lace gown her friend had lent her for the occasion. She had very '80s

Lebanese-style makeup with perfect eyeliner tracing her big almond eyes and mascara over her long lashes finished with a tiny silver star near the corner of her eye. The picture is one of the only memories we managed to salvage from our destroyed home. Both are smiling and seem to be held by the sacredness of the centuries-old stone church they were married in.

Two young people in their twenties find a temporary safe refuge in the confined austerity of Saudi Arabia's harsh desert. My mother, forced to cover herself, felt suffocated by the headscarf that provided a radical contrast to the mini shorts she was used to wearing in Beirut. My father worked long hours in the dust of the sands and the heat of the sun, only to come home late for dinner, where he would gather with friends and drink contraband alcohol. They were living near my grandfather Labib who was working on an architectural project in Saudi Arabia. My father and his father-in-law became close friends during their time in Jeddah and made sure my mother would be safe from Saudi Arabia's "morality police," who targeted and harassed women and made them cover their bodies.

My mother was pregnant with me at that time. Bored beyond comprehension, forced to stay home since women weren't allowed out without a man to chaperone them, she began cleaning the house to keep herself busy—a way to channel her fear and anxiety and extreme boredom. Every day she would clean a part of the home in depth and with great dedication. One day, while wearing shorts and a tank top, she began cleaning the tall windows of the apartment that overlooked the city. While standing on a chair, she elongated her body to reach the top of the glass to pull the dust under her rag to the floor, where the windows ended. After a while working diligently cleaning the large windows, she began to notice a crowd standing below the apartment building. Looking more carefully at the crowd to better understand what was happening, she realized with horror that men were gathered under her building to watch her body move up and down while she cleaned the widows in her shorts and tank top. Taken by a wave of both shame and fear, she stepped away from the windows, closed the curtains, and collapsed on the couch laughing and crying all at once. Her body became a field of battle for the external gaze—violated by their lust and whistles and violated by the "Haram police." Both desired and vilified. A war raging on the soil of her body.

When she was nine months pregnant with me, she wore her abaya open, letting her belly peek out, and uncovering her head, unable to take the high heat of Saudi Arabia. Walking in their neighborhood, my mother, father, and grandfather were intercepted by the Morality Police who began hitting my mother with their stick, demanding she cover up. My grandfather rushed in front of her to protect her while my father tried to stop the policemen and ended up receiving the blows that were intended for her. This altercation resulted in the arrest of my grandfather. He was released from jail only a few hours later, but the incident persuaded my mother that she had to return to Beirut to give birth to me. She had never wanted to deliver her child outside her own country, let alone in Saudi Arabia where her body was the battleground of an ideology she did not believe in.

In the fall of 1982, at nine months pregnant, my mother flew with my father back to Beirut. Although the Israeli invasion of Beirut had ended earlier that year, political tensions had begun to escalate in Lebanon at that time with the murder of Bachir Gemayel and the Sabra and Shatila massacres. General unrest among the population led to military attacks and the bombing of all neighborhoods regardless of religion. My mother was in my grandmother's kitchen eating a persimmon when her water broke. She was rushed to the hospital with my father who, despite the rules at the time, insisted on being by her side. Birthing without anesthesia while bombs are falling, making do with limited resources, no water or electricity, is sadly the reality of all women birthing newborns in times of war—back when I was born, and now in many countries around the world including Occupied Palestine, the Democratic Republic of the Congo, and Sudan.

She gave birth with the sounds of the bombs raining down on us both. I do not consciously remember this moment, but it is a memory stored in my body. While bodies were being dismembered by the weight of the bombs falling on their homes, my mother was pushing with her own young body opening to make way for me. She was sewn back together without the necessary medication to numb the pain. She had only a few days to recover before she and my father and I had to flee from the bombs. Making sure her daughter would be born in Beirut was a form of assurance that one day we'd be back. She chose a foreign (French) name for me because she also knew that the war wasn't going to end soon, and that we'd have to live in the West. No matter how far we ran, and how much effort my parents put into hiding our collective wounds behind the mountain of shame, those wounds would be almost impossible to shake.

Collective trauma outlives war and becomes practically impossible to release. Unlearning war is an ongoing process that requires a long period of safety before the wounds can open up and begin healing. Healing is a painful process. In unlearning the wars I lived through and have continued to experience, I initially found myself called to prayer through the religion I grew up with. Concepts such as post-traumatic stress disorder require a "post" era, which for many of us is only a short break before more violence erupts. Dr. Zainab Asad has explained this concept from the Palestinian experience, where the "post" in post-traumatic stress disorder never happens.

The genocide that began in earnest in the fall of 2023, continuing over 100 years of colonial violence, has been uninterrupted for almost a year at the time of publishing, murdering hundreds of thousands of people, half of whom were children. There might not be a Gaza by the time this book comes out, or a Beirut as the Israeli army is claiming it as theirs under the ideology of the "Promised Land." The war never leaves the body alone; it takes generations to shake off and release the harm wars cause infants, children, teenagers, adults, and elders. It is a vicious poison that penetrates every aspect of the mind, muscles, organs, and spirit. Diseases develop from having experienced war and from being exposed to the pollution it generates.

War forced me to grow up quickly and for my body to contract like a fist at every loud sound. The number of casualties is hard to calculate. Many died under the rubble in Lebanon after the Israeli invasion in 1982, the year my mother gave birth to me. Fifteen thousand people were killed by the Israeli invading forces. Under the siege, no water or food was allowed in as civilians were brutally murdered. Four hundred thousand people were displaced, rendering them houseless and leaving their families and descendants to struggle with intergenerational poverty. The numbers were often refuted by the Israeli government. That, paired with the racist claim that Arabs are animals and that "they exaggerate," discredited any and all real numbers coming from the Lebanese Red Cross, foreign surgeons who were on the ground, or any foreign groups, including UNRWA, who were immediately labeled as "terrorist sympathizers."

"Not *that* many of you died, and if you did die, you deserved it because you dared to rebel against the colonial power"—so goes the settler-invader narrative. Lebanese and Palestinians are accustomed to that form of gaslighting and shaming. The way we healed and unlearned from the wars, over and over again, was through music and storytelling. And although the history books may be written by the occupying forces who dominated the region, the songs and stories carry the truth. The songs and stories recall the tales from our perspective and honor the deaths of the many who perished anonymously and, in their death, were erased and denied the basic human dignity to count, to matter. This form of erasure delays the unlearning of the war that is recorded in our collective memory—not being able to properly mourn the dead and build new infrastructures over the bodies of the ones buried under the rubble.

The ghost town that was Beirut post-1982 remained a haunted ground for years until the first contractors came and decided to remove the rubble and rebuild Lebanon. Songs were made about rebuilding Lebanon, greener and greener, and the defiant spirits of many were revived. Yet in our collective memory, much of our realities were buried under the Mountain of Trauma and would remain there until the next generation, curious and bright-eyed, would begin to ask questions.

"How many people died in Lebanon during the war?"

To which, "We don't want to talk about the people who died, let's talk about those who lived," would be the answer.

The war, whether talked about or not, remained in the bodies of the next generation, and the one after that. I have observed in my own children how their bodies contract like a fist at the sound of a loud plane. They have nightmares of war though they have never lived through a war. One of my own recurring nightmares is of a helicopter with Israeli soldiers hovering in front of my window in my home, blasting the glass off and entering the house with their automatic weapons, hunting me and my family down and brutally killing every one of us. The sound of the helicopter is felt through heavy vibrations in my body while asleep. Waking up covered in sweat, I tell myself, "I am not afraid, I am not afraid," a mantra I repeat over and over until I am, indeed, not afraid. Not afraid of death. Not afraid of terror. But expecting it.

From our early childhood, we were politicized and knew that we were under occupation, that the military in our streets were not there to protect us. In fact, they were there to hurt us, separate us from our families, and kill us. We were aware that our neighbor who had lost her son, kidnapped by the occupation, would probably never return. We knew that if we were to be kidnapped, our bodies would not survive the violence we would have to endure. We saw blood, and some of our friends lost limbs. We witnessed the neighbor's daughter's hair turn completely white due to the shock of her home exploding. We experienced the shelters, hunger, and thirst, and the sadness of our elders. We knew how to understand the big difficult words and the simplicity of it all: the occupation wanted the land, the land had precious resources. We didn't know to call them resources, but we knew what they were. We knew that our own hurt was nothing in comparison with the hurt of all the innocent people who died horrible deaths. We believed that if one was hurting, we were all hurting. That our own pain was nothing in comparison with the pain of the families broken by the war. That our discomfort was nothing in comparison with the discomfort of the young siblings who lived under the highway without their mother or father who were killed in the war. That what we had was a blessing to share. We knew that foreign powers, not knowing how to name them, didn't have our best interest in mind.

We saw blood and empty shelves in every store. We knew money was nothing but paper, and if nothing was left to buy, money didn't have any value. It couldn't buy your dignity or bring your friend back from the dead. We understood geopolitics from the tears our parents held back, and from the rage that followed in which our bodies paid the price. We knew their impatience had deeper roots in injustice, where they had to grow faster than their age, just like us, and that we somehow became their parents at times. Nurturing our own parents. Making sure they did not despair. Holding their hands as they mourned. And not putting any of our own sadness on them, but instead trying to appease their suffering. The selflessness of becoming nothing. Unlearning the war meant not attaching ourselves to anything, not religion or identity, not home or belongings, not even community. All would disappear. And what's left of you when you lose everything?

War made our spirits stronger.

I am nothing
I wrote a poem but please know I am not a poet
I'm nothing,
Our people have been erased to nothing
Called animals and children of darkness
Don't they know?
Don't they know that the very darkness of the womb
Is where life begins?
And the animals hold universal intelligence
Yet we are crushed under the rubbles of our very
                              existence
Erased
Mocked
Dismembered
Ravaged for our resources,
Our food,
Our culture
Erased.
I am nothing,
Under the soil in the darkness of humanity is where
my soul lies
It is where I saw Universe
That is where I know death
The same door which brought me here: birth
We are crushed under our land, in the very soil
                    that has made us
There is no separation between us,
& Soil,
& Water

& air
Our last breath still floats on this Earth
Feeds the trees
Our bodies decompose in our soil
Feeds the earth
From the river to the sea
And they tremble like leaves
Brutalize us,
Try to ye2ta3oulna naffasna [kill our breathing soul]
They fear these words
Water & sea
From the river that nourishes us
They fear Water
To the sea that feeds us
They fear life
They fear darkness
They fear light
I am not a poet
I am nothing
Our people are nothing
To the West
In our nothingness we become everything
We become Earth
We become air
Soil
Water
The fire of our souls
A flame
That lives forever.

CHAPTER IX

Radical Imagi- nation

Cassette #9: A recorded session of Sam Waymon, Nina Simone's brother, playing the grand piano at my birthday, a night in solidarity with Palestinian Liberation

I wish I knew how it would feel to be free
I wish I could break all the chains holding me
I wish I could say all the things that I should say
Say 'em loud, say 'em clear
For the whole round world to hear

I wish I could share all the love that's in my heart
Remove all the bars that keep us apart
I wish you could know what it means to be me
Then you'd see and agree
That every man should be free

Surviving Wars

If we make it out alive, we will be broken by it all. Wounds that have no words in the English dictionary and that can only be expressed through wailing and screams. Grief so painful no words can begin to describe it, making anyone who witnesses it feel like they have experienced a form of death. Anyone who makes it out alive makes it out broken to bits.

In my personal healing journey, I found solace in the words of Rumi: "The wound is the place where the Light enters you." This sentence is my lifeline, I hold on to it. I visualize light emanating from every part of my body that has been broken by pain.

Western psychology is limited to the individual; it isolates us into a perfect container exploring the depth of a single consciousness, devoid of context and connections. It's an unfruitful exploration for me. My healing journey has taken me places that individualism and Western ideas of healing can't comprehend or reach. The limitations of US-based healing work and concepts of "wellness" ignite a rage in me. Rage at the very idea of all the concepts and words, rage at the exclusion of the experience of Arabs under bombardment, under siege, subjected to colonialism and imperialism that continue to oppress us economically, politically, and environmentally to this day. Before we can even imagine and create a radical future, we must heal our hearts. And before we can heal, we must stop the ongoing violence. How can we heal while wounds are being actively created?

The human spirit is even more resilient than the body, and somehow we are able to heal while still being wounded. And again, this healing must be a healing of the heart. Otherwise the imagination is wounded and limited by the hurt we feel. It's the same observation I noticed in design. If the designer is wounded, in pain, the design will not be open and generous enough to welcome the majority. It's almost impossible. Perhaps art can lend itself to exploring healing, but imagination of radical possible futures and designing possibilities require working from a healed place. We never finish healing, but if we acknowledge our wounds and allow light to enter us, we move into a healed place. Artists and creators who have experienced war, survived it, and find themselves looking at how they can turn their wounds into wisdom by looking at the past and reconciling it with the future are the treasures of a nation.

Collective healing spaces are rare. Under colonial capitalism, most spaces are commercialized and individualized such that healing consists of only an individualistic approach to self-care, reduced to a capitalist transaction. In contrast, true collective healing is about exchange, where care for self takes place in the context of care of others, and meaningful conversations can occur. The wellness industry in the Global North fosters isolation, prioritizing individual care over the idea of collective well-being.

The mythology of individualism positions people above other people, nature, and the environment. This form of hierarchy and categorization of some human lives above others is inherently part of political agendas that reinforce colonial and oppressive regimes around the world, starting in occupied Turtle Island in the so-called United States. The next step in this mythology is to prop up the nation-state as more important than the collective of people it purports to represent, as if the nation-state itself were an individual.

Why do we accept nation-states as inexorable facts, while concepts of Indigenous sovereignty, lives, and culture are "alternative," even "provocative" narratives? Shouldn't it be the opposite? Why should we respect these nation states created by force, built on the bones of Indigenous children? Nations are built on wars and have yet to reckon with the collective, justice-centered healing necessary to move forward toward regenerative and compassionate policies that center on human rights and climate justice. Even in nations such as Canada, where an official "Truth and Reconciliation" process regarding its genocidal history has supposedly happened, almost no actions under that banner have been taken.

I base my theory of radical imagination on the foundations of collective healing as we have established them at Slow Factory, the organization I created with my partner, Colin Vernon. In 2008 we established the name Slow Factory, which speaks to the idea of slowing down factories of oppression, and later in 2012, we launched the project online. Implicit in the underlying assumptions of Slow Factory is that the People are more important than the Nation, that the collective well-being of the people and cultures that make up society are more important than the economic systems ostensibly created to serve them.

Collective care, collective healing, and any framework centering on vulnerable communities who have survived atrocious events must be anchored in radical generosity and dialogue favoring the act of listening compassionately—eradicating the condescending feelings of charity and pity and replacing them with solidarity and kinship. Any idea that continues to linger within facilitators' minds that their culture sits above another's, and above nature itself, must first be dismantled completely. A fundamental unlearning of one of the most basic and harmful repressive narratives that isolate humans from humanity, and subsequently from nature, is a necessary step—in fact, one of the few steps that require an individual inquiry that could later translate into a collective care practice.

Decentering whiteness and Western colonial values in favor of collective care is the work of a lifetime. How can we build a sustainable culture, systems, and infrastructure on the very exploitative cultures that have created climate change by way of oppression and extraction and legalized pollutants and wars? How can we find something left to fight for under these misguided beliefs and limited forms of imagination? The answer may upset those members of the dominant culture who are accustomed to witnessing the world wrapped in comfort from a safe distance.

Centuries of human rights violations in the form of the legalization of pollution by overproduction and over-extraction of resources at the expense of Indigenous cultures around the world have pushed nations into poverty and starvation. Women's bodies have been raped and violated at the same rate the earth has been raped and violated. These aren't generalizations or a vulgar summary of what colonialism is doing to our planet, from Palestine to the Congo by way of Turtle Island and Yemen. These are paradigms many have taken for granted and assumed to be true because this "norm" has been imposed on everyone in the Global North. There is a toxic idea that the countries in the Global North are civilized, clean, and advanced as opposed to the countries in the Global South, which for many years were labeled "Third World" or the "developing world," terms that insinuated they weren't as "evolved" as the Global North.

This framing completely disregards the reason for economic resource disparity. For hundreds of years countries of the Global North have used, as tools of oppression, weapons, torture, and rape along with "educational" campaigns that frame any global Natives as barbaric savages requiring force in order to be "civilized." The goals and results of this dehumanization is to extract resources that enrich the North while impoverishing the South, creating the very disparity between "developed" and "developing" that naturalizes what is a very simple relationship of exploitation. This is an aspect of the colonial-white imagination masquerading as truth where plurality is seen as wrong and conformity is seen as the "we are all the same" paradigm that is the very foundation of settler colonialism. This notion of "universalism" eradicated the differences between people, rendering them illegal. The goal is to assimilate and look the same—or as much as possible—hence the annihilation of Indigenous people around the world and the vilification of any and all alternative medicines, ceremonies, or beliefs that strayed from what is.

In biological terms, it is an anti-biodiversity project that parallels the results of extractions and exploitations to meet standardization methods of production around the world, causing climate change and resulting in great biodiversity loss. Designing linear and highly productive systems prioritizes productivity and speed at the expense of culture, biodiversity, and regeneration of natural resources. In colonial capitalist culture, the notion of productivity is superior to the notion of biodiversity and plurality. In fact, the latter is threatening, which is a difficult realization to make. I'm grateful to have made it during my teenage years when my parents left the comfort of the Global North to return to their land and home in Beirut, where the teachings of my grandparents continue to guide me in stewarding my culture, with an understanding of the world and our deep connection to land.

Lifelong Healing

In healing my wounds, I found myself healing my mother's and her mother's as well. Through my own work in tending to my broken heart, I arrived at the Mountain of Trauma to uncover what it was trying to tell me. I have shattered the harmful stories that have led me to believe fallacies about my own people. With perspective, I later noticed how entire communities would hold the belief that their own culture was evil and enact horrific acts of violence against each other. Colonial indoctrination travels from one generation to another, carrying with it self-loathing mantras and self-destructive tendencies. Witnessing misery, injustice, and violence from birth until today has cemented my relationship with depression and anxiety.

For all who grew up in Lebanon before the end of the war, the paralyzing sound of bombs is recorded in our nervous systems where the rhythm of fear and panic reverberates throughout our lives. Sounds of planes flying low play on a loop in our memories. Fear hardens the body and affects both the tissues and the organs and increases the amount of cortisol and adrenaline in the bloodstream. Wars create compounding tremors in the body and spirit that require collective care and dedicated healing efforts. But like many countries in the Global South, Lebanon doesn't have enough financial support to cover the cost of mental health care to the population of survivors. In fact, gaslighting strategies are often employed in an attempt to diminish the population's pain. Money is invested in distractions like new shopping malls that invite foreign franchises to open shops and feed people burgers to numb the pain. Consumption and impossible European beauty ideals and notions of success are pushed on us in an attempt to erase what happened and show us where to channel our emotions. Xanax and Valium sold over the counter and cheap cigarettes have become the go-to addictions for all. Smoking away the past, marching barefoot to churches dressed in the outfits of saints, fasting, praying in circles, and sacrificing everything we loved for the healing of someone dear.

At school we spent a full day once a month in a monastery hidden in nature where we were forced to remain in total silence while doing chores. We spent hours doing community services and chanting prayers. A fifteen-minute confession was mandatory, and the younger priests would encourage us to express ourselves, to release what was in our heart. It was a form of therapy with the addition of God's forgiveness and the priest's assurance that we were now pure and liberated from pain or temptation. Confessions began with "I am sorry, I have sinned ..." or "Please forgive me, for I have sinned ..." Whatever the sin was, whether it was our fault or not, we took responsibility for it and assumed it was ours to carry to redemption. We were not mere victims of our situation, we were responsible for it. After spending a full day in silence executing tiring chores, we were relieved to have this moment with the priests, and many of us left the oratory in tears but with a sense of release and freedom. How wonderful to know that God would forgive us pretty much anything we would have the courage to admit.

During the many coffee ceremonies, our aunties and neighbors would confess to one another many horrific things they couldn't carry alone anymore. We all became the witness of each other's pains and sins. We would drink coffee, eat sweets, and vent, release, confess, and hold each other while we processed, mourned, admitted fault, and took responsibility for our stories. Even children were encouraged to share what was in their hearts. Coffee ceremonies were sacred and held a place in our society for collective healing and collective care.

We were each other's compassionate witnesses, not only listening with intent but feeding each other and offering advice, arguing then laughing and teasing. These were the ways in which we as a community processed the horrendous events we'd witnessed and survived. We found solace in each other. If someone was mourning, we would listen and offer our hearts; we helped each other carry the pain of loss and grief. We cooked for each other and helped each other process the unimaginable pain we all felt. We would make each other laugh. Acts of radical generosity. Every time I leave these communal spaces of care and reciprocity, a part of me is separated from my roots.

And where I left these spaces to go was, of course, back to the Global North—both the ultimate source of the turmoil and wars and unrest that punish my country, and the place of physical safety to which we were forced to flee. I remember scenes of physical pain and mental turmoil, lying on the floor; a quiet snow day wrapped my peaceful Montreal apartment in silence. Here in the Global North my mind felt uprooted and I felt alone. Healing in the West was offered to me as a free service at university in Montreal where I was able to schedule time to speak with a psychologist once a week to address issues I was dealing with. Being afforded the opportunity to receive a formal diagnosis and hopefully heal the mysterious, haunting pain damaging my well-being was thrilling. I wanted to talk to someone, to have a witness, to let people in the West know what it was like, what their countries were creating in our world, and to find solace in their compassion.

I booked a session with a therapist, a lady in her forties or fifties, a Québécoise with short hair and a round, nurturing figure. I spent my first session sobbing; I couldn't utter a full sentence. What came out of me was incomprehensible. The doctor looked at me, just like I had seen them do in movies, and took notes in silence. Her office was filled with books and papers everywhere, a typical scene, except the walls were painted dark blue, and the windowsills dark green with potted plants sitting on them. The doctor stared at me without telling what she was thinking or what she had written. The validation and vindication I dreamed of was nowhere to be found.

In the second session, I made a monumental effort

to not burst into tears, to speak in full sentences, and to share as much as I could until I fell silent. I stared back at her, waiting for a reaction or advice. Where was the advice that would allow me to refine my position? Silence. I asked her what she'd written. She looked at me and responded, "These are my notes, you can continue if you feel compelled." She was so proper and restrained. How was I supposed to express myself with these constraints? I was talking to myself in front of a total stranger who was not invested in my life at all. How extremely isolating. I continued sharing for a little while until the therapist interrupted me to say we were "at time." I awkwardly stopped, collected my belongings, and thanked her. I rushed out and burst into tears. I ran into a local store and purchased a chocolate bar to eat the remainder of my emotions.

There weren't any coffee ceremonies for me to go to in Montreal. Coffee came in a to-go cup. I drank it alone outside in the cold while smoking from a ten-dollar pack of cigarettes, thinking about everything that was haunting me. Healing came in a lot of different forms there. I could enroll in a yoga class, which was becoming popular and practiced everywhere. Separated from its spiritual context, it was sterilized into neat polyester pants and mats and taught by white instructors who spoke softly yet firmly and emphasized performance. We ended with an "Om" and a "Namaste." Leaving yoga classes, I felt a sense of self, a sense of release, yet I continued to feel disconnected and uprooted. Something continued to be missing from every single modality I was invited to explore.

In this quiet privilege I was now afforded, my duty was to heal as best I could so I could be of service to my community in Lebanon and around the world. But how could I be of service if I was unable to address the issues that resulted in me contracting and closing down on myself? Alone in my living room I would make myself coffee and sit with fear. I spent time sharing my coffee ceremony with fear herself, listening to all she had to say to me— true or false, it didn't matter. I allowed fear to confess to me what I was suspicious of. She shared generously until she became tired of repeating herself. The stronger I remained in not embodying her worries and concerns, the better I became at witnessing them and releasing them if I didn't agree with them.

Fear was no longer in control of me in those moments. I became the mother of my fear and allowed her to express herself, finally, after she'd spent years in silence. I listened to her and was able to discern what resonated with me and what was completely irrelevant and had expired. I spent a lot of time alone looking deeply within myself, carefully unknotting hurt that was stored deep within the labyrinth of my subconscious. I kept fasting, as I had learned to do in Lebanon, sacrificing food and emptying my body to better feel my spirit.

Years later, on a journey to Hawai'i through Slow Factory's Deep Ecology program, I learned that the concept of the glass half empty or half full was all wrong, a false dichotomy as so much of Western culture is based on.

We were invited to an undisclosed area reserved for Indigenous Hawai'ians with the guidance of Kanaka Maoli Kūpuna (elders), keepers of knowledge and wisdom. An elder asked us if we think our cup is half full or half empty. Some raised their hands for half full and others for half empty, and she looked at us and laughed. "It's always full! It is full of both water and Spirit, the cup is never empty."

This new perspective on such a tired metaphor replenished my soul. I always aim to be full of spirit. As much as I can, I invite my spirit back in to take control of my vessel, my body. I make sure my spirit has its needs met as much as possible, though I have famously ignored it and hurt it. And at times, when it spoke to me, I purposefully pretended I didn't hear—only to find out the hard way that I should have taken an umbrella on a day that seemed sunny when I left the house, or that I should have kept a certain comment to myself. I should have listened to my spirit when it said, "Don't trust this person," or "Don't go there." But Western therapy doesn't necessarily teach you any of this. It listens to you talk about the same things out loud and patiently hopes you, alone, individually, will gather the evidence you need to move forward. The individualistic approach of healing can be sterile and isolating, sending many to discover alternative ways to complement this sometimes costly healing method.

I was very fortunate to have experienced it in Canada, where taxes actually support basic public services such as health care, including mental health care. This is not the case in most countries, yet it should be. Imagine if budgets were spent on healing and providing communities with care instead of providing funds to bomb, displace, and pollute abroad. What do we get from economies of war but broken souls? What if we were able to receive the funding needed to create new spaces for collective and individual care, where mental health and spiritual health are prioritized? Where wounded people are given the opportunity to heal and to explore their personal healing journeys? Where our spiritual and mental health is seen as sacred and where collectively we encourage one another to heal and explore ourselves?

Lifelong Unlearning

We must allow ourselves to imagine, radically imagine, what can exist for our highest good. Otherwise we won't be able to progress as a species on this planet. If we only look at what is realistic and possible, we will stagnate. What if scientists had listened to those who couldn't imagine the possibilities of space travel? We wouldn't have been able to witness it in our lifetime. In 1962 the Lebanese Space Program was founded by the Lebanese Rocket Society, a nongovernmental organization that emerged from the Haigazian College Rocket Society founded by Manoug Manougian in 1960 upon his arrival in Lebanon. Manoug was of Armenian origin; his family fled the 1915 genocide of Armenians to Jerusalem, Palestine, where he was born in 1935. He studied in Texas and then moved to Lebanon to teach at Haigazian College.

His work was deeply politically aware; he was known to write editorials advocating awareness about the Armenian genocide, and coauthored and produced a four-hour documentary called *The Genocide Factor: The Human Tragedy*, which aired on PBS. The Rocket Society successfully launched a series of suborbital "Cedar rockets," which gained attention from the media and the public, leading to its sponsorship by the Lebanese government at the time. Renamed by Lebanese president Fouad Chehab as the Lebanese Space Program, it produced the first rockets of the Arab World.

The Cedar rockets had equal power to the rockets of the French that were colonizing Lebanon at the time, leading Western governments to ultimately forbid Lebanon from pursuing the project. French president, Charles de Gaulle, warned President Chehab in a personal letter that since Lebanese scientists had managed to prove their achievements and match those of the Europeans and American scientists, the Lebanese government would become a target by foreign powers if the space program were to continue to reach further scientific progress in building and launching rockets.

These forms of censorship and sabotage executed by foreign powers to further their colonial grip over Lebanon infiltrated the culture and psyche of many and became internalized values Lebanese people held against themselves. This event, among many others, reinforced a belief in the Lebanese people that no matter how far they progress, they will never receive the level of acknowledgment that Europeans and Americans receive. In fact, the Lebanese people were told that continuing with scientific research and progress would endanger the entire culture.

Unlearning these limiting beliefs imposed by colonial oppression begins with identifying the patterns of these beliefs. The first foundational pattern is the emotional disdain one may have against their own kin, culture, or traditions. Anyone close to the land is considered less than more modern urban people, therefore the labor needed for the land is looked down upon. Loss of cultural and traditional knowledge results in separation and disdain leading to a culture that relies more and more on imported goods and prefabricated disposable products that contribute to climate change and eventual economic collapse (in the case of Lebanon).

The second pattern that must be unlearned, to facilitate the radical imagination that is vital for collective liberation, is the idea that traditional culture and ancient wisdom are irrelevant in comparison with modern ways of thinking and living. This pattern is the refusal to engage and connect with traditional knowledge, labeling it as either irrelevant or discredited by "modern" science and standards coming from the Westernized world that are positioned as superior to Indigenous wisdom. This misunderstanding creates an imbalance in our cultures and contributes to the erasure of our own systems of understanding, our language and culture, as well as our relationship to our traditions and history. This pattern has been largely adopted by what I call "the lost generation," or folks born in the '50s who lived under colonial rule and were raised in colonial schools in Lebanon where their education was primarily based on a European model. This indoctrination was reinforced by the dissemination and popularity of European music and American and European cinema. Lebanese culture at the time stood in direct contrast to the Western narratives making their way into the collective psyche that promoted modernity and Western beauty standards. This Western messaging influenced an entire generation to adopt foreign cultural standards at the expense of their own, which they began to despise, continuing this generations-long tradition of cultural erasure and self-loathing imposed by colonial rule.

The third pattern that must be unlearned is the notion that we must shrink ourselves to survive, that we must self-censor or adopt the attitude of the oppressor and censor others who are being loud and noticeable, or behaving in a way that some consider to be "out-there" or just different. One who believes we must erase ourselves to survive would ask someone to quiet down, warning them not to attract attention. This pattern can also show up in a mother or other authority figure who tells their children not to speak Arabic, not to wear traditional clothes, and to blend in as much as possible so as to not attract danger. This is especially the case in a violent climate where people are murdered point-blank in the streets for speaking their language or wearing a keffiyeh or traditional wear. This tendency to self-erase is common in immigrant communities as well as communities under occupation. On the one hand, occupation must be resisted by any means necessary, and on the other, a group of people afraid for their loved ones become ready to compromise anything about themselves in order to sustain their lives and the lives of their communities.

This tendency to shrink to survive takes generations to unlearn. It creates an inner devil's advocate, or worse, an impostor syndrome in anyone who dares to be born with an irreverent spirit that calls for joyful defiance. Are we allowed to cause so much trouble? Communities who are being subjugated by colonial powers internalize the abuse and are then held responsible for causing the conflict in the first place. This is a pernicious colonial tactic that is widely employed around the world. Communities and individuals battling with self-erasure can unwittingly or even intentionally promote "horizontal hostilities" (as we refer to them in activist circles). They end up policing family and community members by cautioning them to tone down their opinions or self-expression. All these patterns demand of us to shrink, contract, and disappear. We are told that this will keep us "safe."

These misunderstandings do not lead us to liberation. When perpetuated, they distort and often reduce our ability to expand, imagine, and create. The more we unconsciously uphold them, the more harm we end up doing to ourselves and, by extension, to others. Other patterns adopted by subjugated communities to survive colonial oppression are patterns surrounding success and status.

What we consider to be successful and of value are an imitation of Western/patriarchal/capitalist/white cultural values. These values center on money and individualism at the expense of community-centered cultures of care and art. Art, literature, and the critical role of the intellectual are all rendered obsolete in a culture that prizes order and obedience.

Money and success, two sides of the same coin, influence families, individuals, and societies to make decisions that contribute to the erasure of traditional knowledge systems, the destruction rather than preservation of Indigenous culture, as well as a disregard for the stewardship of ancient Indigenous wisdom. This kind of erasure feeds the second pattern by contributing to the erasure of one's identity, one's connection to culture and traditions. Other patterns revolve around beauty standards and the plastic surgery business that provides physical alterations for subjugated women and men to alter their bodies to resemble and assimilate as much as possible with the dominant culture.

It is the opposition to this kind of insidious and omnipresent cultural erasure that has informed my work with my organization Slow Factory—a body of work representing hundreds of classes, seminars, workshops, events, and conferences exposing these patterns of oppression and providing pathways toward lifelong unlearning and the act of recalibrating one's identity and culture and reorienting our roots toward collective liberation. This brings me to the last pattern—the ultimate separation—which is between humans and nature. The belief that some people (belonging to the dominant, colonizing culture) sit above others who are deemed lesser also supports the belief that people are above nature, which is perceived to be nothing but a bunch of rocks, water, and resources at the disposal of the ruling class. This belief that people are above nature justifies the exploitation of both land and people and disregards pollution and the destruction of natural environments.

Radical Imagination

If you were given all the means possible where nothing is too hard or too complex to create, what would you do? How would we cocreate a world that is both good for people (all people) and good for our planet? I have asked this question to hundreds of people throughout the course of my work. This is a participatory design framework that is meant to create a sort of tabula rasa (in philosophy, the complete removal of all constraints, barriers, preconceived ideas on a given topic) and open all the roads in order to create new pathways toward a given solution. What if no amount of support were too large and all constraints were removed? What would you create?

Responses are unique to each individual and each participant, depending on who they are and where they are located around the world. However, some similarities in the categories of responses could be comparable or at least serve as a common denominator for our exploration.

When I think of this question and allow myself to enter a meditative state where in fact anything is both possible and available to me to cocreate and design a possible future, I end up gravitating toward a few nonnegotiable guidelines around which I center my work. The guidelines revolve around community and nature as one and the same, or if separation is demanded, as two interlaced concepts that feed off each other and that cannot be disturbed in the solution-making or ideation process.

Communities can also be understood as the most vulnerable at the heart. Ideation is grounded in compassion and care; inspiration must flow from a state of inner peace and joy as much as possible. Anger, pain, sadness, and oppressive feelings must be looked at, explored, cared for, and nurtured in the first phase of the process, which revolves around collective healing spaces to achieve a sense of radical imagination. Solving difficult and complex issues can and must invite a sense of play and child-like possibilities. Healing is the foundation of imagination and collective liberation. The framework that guides my process is centering communities and nature, interwoven as one. My process also includes the exploration of geographies outside nation-states and political agendas. Why? Because we are looking at a radical possible future rather than incremental adjustments in a problematic and rotten system. This process allows us to expand outside of current harmful systems of oppression toward radical care, radical generosity, and the irreverent expression of our freedom.

At Slow Factory we have been doing what we call *Applied Utopia*, which means creating and building a multiracial, multiethnic, multifaith, multicultural society. We must transform the homogenous systems the current world we exist in is built on and explore pluriversal systems that invite multiplicity. *Applied Utopia* requires exploring the following to radically transform ourselves and the world we live in:

1. How can we redesign decision-making to create a strategic system that centers on the most vulnerable and empowers everyone to take leadership in specific areas of expertise?

2. How can we embrace a culture of differences and multiplicity without weaponizing differences or division but rather focusing on shared visions for collective care?

3. How can we embrace conflict and differentiate conflict from harmful, abusive relationships, and learn conflict resolution skills as an important part of creating a world where different cultures come together without erasing one another?

4. How can we design systems centered around grieving, healing, and collective care to explore trade-offs, negotiations, and reckoning with the harmful past and the collective wounds it has left behind?

5. How can we establish a deep relationship with repairing the harms of anti-Blackness and take an introspective approach to misogyny, ableism, prejudice against Arabs, and any forms of oppression against any group that has been normalized by the current dominant culture?

6. How can we develop a deep relationship with creativity and explore participatory frameworks that allow us to cocreate together?

Each of these explorations is deeply inspired by the chapters in this book and countless stories that have been shared with me by my elders and the many Indigenous elders I have encountered along the way, as well as the adventures and misadventures I've personally experienced while traveling the world, living in Lebanon before and after the civil war, and living in Canada as a refugee. These explorations are also inspired by my outsider status and my close observation of Western society and culture.

Radical imagination is possible when we can repair our relationship with creativity and imperfection. It is imperative that we create and collaborate together as a community and build a culture of forgiveness. Mistakes happen and perfectionism is one of the poisoned fruits of colonial culture. It completely castrates any idea that needs to fail a few times before becoming viable. Our relationship with failure is calling for reconciliation. How can we unlearn self-punishment and explore compassion for ourselves if we can't allow ourselves to make mistakes and recover from them? We can't innovate if we aren't in a position to try, fail, and learn from the mistakes that created the failure in the first place.

I personally have failed many times throughout my career. I have self-sabotaged and punished myself. I have judged myself so harshly that I have sometimes wished I weren't alive just because of a mistake. Mistakes can be expensive, but they cost you the ability to learn if they can't be dissected and ultimately accepted. Your ability to learn—and unlearn—is profoundly valuable. Radical imagination is both a personal effort as well as a collective one. For the purpose of this book, and as the final chapter, I open the question to all. If there were no constraints and if there were no budget too big, what would you do?

Photo by Sunny Shokrae

Céline is a Lebanese-Canadian designer, writer, speaker, and advocate working at the intersection of environmental and social justice. She speaks four languages, is an educator, strategist, and mother.

As the founder of Slow Factory, a 501(c)(3) nonprofit, Céline addresses climate justice and social inequity. Slow Factory hosts Study Hall, a sustainability literacy conference, One X One, a fashion-focused science-driven incubator, and a material science lab.

Her works have received many awards: Slow Factory's Open Edu has received an award from Harvard for innovation in education; Slow Factory Labs has been awarded a Fast Company Innovation by Design award, and has been a finalist in many global design and innovation competitions.

Céline's advocacy extends to her involvement with the Council of Progressive International, MIT Media Lab, and AIGA NY's Board of Directors.